How a Mountain of Fire and a Rebellious Cherub
Altered History in Heaven and on Earth

PERRY STONE

CHRONICLES

OF THE

SACRED

MOUNTAIN

Revealing the Mysteries of Heaven's
Past, Present and Future

CHRONICLES
OF THE
SACRED
MOUNTAIN

CHRONICLES OF THE SACRED MOUNTAIN
Published by: Voice of Evangelism Outreach Ministries
P. O. Box 3595
Cleveland, TN 37320
www.voe.org
423.478.3456

Unless otherwise noted, Scripture quotations are from the King James
Version of the Bible.

Scripture quotations marked NKJV are from the New King James
Version of the Bible Copyright © 1979, 1980, 1982 by Thomas
Nelson, Inc., Publishers. Used by permission.

ISBN 978-0-9785920-7-3
First Edition Printing: August, 2015

Cover design illustration and layout by Michael Dutton
Angel wings by http://cocacolagirlie.deviantart.com
Matte painting by Bobby Myers

CONTENTS

The Mystery of Ages Past

H AVE YOU EVER looked at the heavens and wondered: where does it all end? Or does it end? What is out there in the universe? What is beyond the universe?

From childhood through my early teens, three seemingly insignificant events are imprinted in my mind to this day. At age five, the first funeral I ever attended was at my dad's rural church in Big Stone Gap, Virginia. Imagine my confusion, as believers peered into the lifeless face of the departed and proclaimed, "He's not here, he is with the Lord!" I thought, "No, he's not with the Lord, he's in that big box."

This event was branded in my mind for several years, until I heard sermons that explained how the soul and spirit depart the physical body at the moment of death, and how the righteous spirits are taken to be with the Lord (2 Cor. 5:6-8).

Many years later my father, Fred Stone, preached about heaven. Later that night as I lay in bed, I opened the curtains to the bedroom window, stared up at the stars, and attempted to count them. Then I thought, "What is beyond all of that starry space? Does it ever end? How can it end? And if it does end, then what's beyond the end?" The concept of *endless space* staggered my imagination.

Around age thirteen, I was pondering the length of eternity. Is eternity a never ending time in which you are forever stuck at the same age with no more birthdays? In my young mind I imagined how *bored* I would be living that long without a break, as I viewed heaven as some mystical land on the edge of space where angels rested on puffy clouds and baby cherubs floated around strumming golden harps, singing hymns to white-robed elderly people with hands clasped below their chins in the prayer position, and greeting each other with a solemn, "Hello, my brother," or "Good day, sister." That day I breathed a prayer and asked God if He would turn me into a gold brick or something of His choice when I got bored, because as a child and teen, I despised boredom. (Of course, I have long since canceled this childish request).

Fast forward to age sixteen, the age that God called me into ministry. It was my high school sophomore year and, at times, I requested an early release from class to travel to a church and preach. When students discovered I was a young preacher, they began to harass me. During one class, a rather rebellious boy named Bud spoke up and said, "Preacher man, what will you do when you die and find out there's no heaven?" I was always quick to answer and replied, "Bud, what will you do when you die and find out there's a hell?"

This mocker actually provoked me to deeper study. That day I began detailed research from the Bible and science to prove that the heaven of the Bible exists. From this research, at age eighteen I began to preach a message titled, "Heaven: Location, Destination," which for many years became my most requested message and has been called a classic by early ministry partners.

In my twenties, I was further struck with the burning desire to understand the mysteries of the Bible after learning that there was an "ageless past" before Adam's creation. For some reason, I never heard that taught in the church when I was growing up. I discovered that angels were created long before the first man Adam, and that Satan, the highest ranking angel, fell and was cast from heaven during an unknown gap of time between the initial creation in Genesis 1:1 and the chaotic earth alluded to in Genesis 1:2.

I began to dig into Scripture to understand the heavenly *position* and *assignment* of Satan before his violent expulsion from heaven. I sought answers to five questions for which I could not recall ever hearing an explanation:

- God created the heavens along with the earth; but what did He create *in heaven* in the beginning? (Gen. 1:1)

- Who were the *morning stars* that sang together when the foundation of the earth was laid? (Job 38:7)

- Satan fell because of pride over his *beauty;* so what specific features made him so beautiful? (Ezek. 28:12, 17)

- What was Satan doing in heaven that inspired *one-third* of the angels to follow him in rebellion? (Rev. 12:4)

- What were the *stones of fire* that Satan walked on, and what was their link to his expulsion from heaven? (Ezek. 28:14-16)

While pondering these and other mysteries, I was ministering in Texas, where I spoke to a pastor who had been a professional jeweler. He commented that it requires both *fire* and *pressure* to create gemstones. Illumination began to enter my mind and unlock the secrets to understanding the fall of Satan and the reason Satan's kingdom hates the earthly Jerusalem. This *anatomy of eternity past* will cut through the veil of ages past—ages that began with the mysteries of the *stones of fire*—and their connection to one anointed cherub.

You are about to delve into a mystery of ages past and eternity future, a mystery that will unlock the concealed wonders of heaven from a different perspective. Several chapters in this book contain recent research, as there are entire sections that I have never placed in print before. I pray you will glean new understanding of heaven, of the mystery of Satan's fall, and of the reason Jerusalem was chosen as the city of redemption. This entire true story becomes the *chronicles of the sacred mountain!*

Always moving toward eternity,
Perry Stone, Jr.

CHAPTER 1

Visions of God

THE HEBREW PROPHETS are a distinguished coalition of inspired men, many of whom claimed to have seen visions of God. One such seer was a controversial figure named Balaam. In Numbers chapter 24, Balaam was identified as an Old Testament prophet who compromised and abused his prophetic gift for personal gain (Jude 11). He fell into a trance and saw a vision of God:

> "And Balaam lifted up his eyes, and he saw Israel abiding in his tents according to their tribes; and the spirit of God came upon him. And he took up his parable, and said, Balaam the son of Beor hath said, and the man whose eyes are open hath said: He hath said, which heard the words of God, which saw the vision of the Almighty, falling into a trance, but having his eyes open."
>
> – NUMBERS 24:2-4

> "And he took up his parable, and said, Balaam the son of Beor hath said, and the man whose eyes are open hath said: He hath said, which heard the words of God, and knew the knowledge of the most High, which saw the vision of the Almighty, falling into a trance, but having his eyes open."
>
> – NUMBERS 24:15-16

In the Torah account, Moses wrote that Balaam spoke of seeing God while in a *trance*. In the above verses the word *trance* is not in the original Hebrew text, but was added by the translators for better readability in English. However, both passages speak of Balaam seeing a "vision" with his "eyes open," which is called an *open vision*. A vision enables the seer to peer beyond the heavenly veil, open a door into the spirit world, and pierce beyond the natural world into the celestial cosmos. When a Biblical seer or prophet such as Daniel saw a vision or prophetic symbolism of future events, it occurred by one of two methods—either a *sleeping vision* or an *open vision*.

A *sleeping vision* emerges when the visionary is fully asleep; yet the imagery they see appears three-dimensional and full of color, with all five senses of the seer—seeing, hearing smelling, touching and even tasting—being fully alert, just as though the visionary is fully awake and encountering a literal experience. Daniel spoke of receiving a "night vision" (Dan. 2:19), and a "vision by night" (Dan. 7:2), which was a visitation from God so clear, that the images were burnt into his mind while he was yet sleeping.

An example of an *open vision* is observed in Daniel 10. On the 24th day of the first month, Daniel and his companions were beside the river Hiddekel (the Tigris), when his eyes turned to see a vision of a man he described, recorded in Daniel 10:

> "...behold a certain man clothed in linen, whose waist was girded with gold of Uphaz! His body was like beryl, his face like the appearance of lightning, his eyes like torches of fire, his arms and feet like burnished bronze in color, and the sound of his words like the voice of a multitude."
>
> – DAN. 10:5-6 (NKJV)

In the story, Daniel's companions *saw* nothing, but *felt* the presence of this angelic messenger as we read:

> "...a great terror came over them and they fled to hide themselves"
>
> – DAN. 10:7 (NKJV)

Night visions during sleep are common among Biblical prophets, but an open vision, which transports a seer from the present scene to another dimension in an instant, is a unique and rare experience. Ezekiel experienced this, along with the Apostle John when he was a political prisoner surrounded by a watery sea on a desolate, rocky volcanic island called Patmos. John was suddenly "in the Spirit on the Lord's day" (Rev. 1:10). Immediately he was *caught up* into the heavenly temple and later penned his apocalyptic scroll, revealing the things that *are*, and that *will be* in the future (Rev. 1:19).

Balaam's experience would be classified as a *trance*, as he saw a *vision* with his *eyes opened*. For a prophetic seer or prophet to escape out of his visible surroundings, cut through the veil of eternity, and make the invisible visible, there must be a lifting or removing of some form of spiritual scales that cover the human eyes and blind the mind, just as Elisha's servant could not see the invisible army of horses and chariots of fire until Elisha prayed for his servant's eyes to be opened (2 Kings 6:15-17). To see the invisible, some type of blinders must lift from your eyes, and to hear the voice of God, the inner ears of the human spirit must be opened (Rev. 2:7).

As for Balaam, at one time he was in tune in three areas:

- He heard the *words* of God, meaning his *spiritual ears* were opened (Num. 24:15-16)

- He had *knowledge* of God, meaning that his *spiritual mind* was opened (Num. 24:15-16)

- He saw the *vision* of God with his eyes opened, meaning his *spiritual eyes* were opened (Num. 24:2-4).

From birth, some people seem sensitive to spiritual matters and are able to discern activity in the spirit realm, both good and evil. Dreaming dreams that conceal the future or give spiritual instructions and warnings to others can be a gift and even be passed down through the family, as though part of the DNA.

Abraham encountered God through a vision (Gen. 15:1). There is no Biblical record of Abraham's son Isaac experiencing either a dream or a vision; however, Isaac's son Jacob tapped into the gift of spiritual dreaming on several occasions. He saw angels on a ladder reaching into heaven (Gen. 28:12) and received angelic instructions after twenty years in exile in Syria, where an angel told him to journey back to Canaan Land to see his father Isaac before he passed (Gen. 31:10-18).

Jacob had twelve sons, but only one—his favorite son Joseph—had the dream gift. His dreams revealed future events that would impact his family's destiny. Both of Joseph's dreams predicted that his eleven brothers would one day pay him homage and bow before him (Gen. 37:5-11). At age seventeen, Joseph openly spoke of the dreams and incited the jealousy of his ten older brothers, who mocked him and spitefully sold him as a slave. Then afterwards, the brothers concealed their actions by presenting to their father Joseph's multi-colored coat covered in goat's blood (Gen. 37:28-33).

However, twenty years later during a global famine, Joseph's brothers traveled to Egypt and purchased grain as they unknowingly bowed before Joseph, who was then second-in-command over Egypt's economy and agriculture (Gen 42:6). Thus, God can and does make His will known to men through spiritual visions and dreams.

THE SPIRIT WORLD AND FIRE

Why is God *invisible*, and what makes Him, at times, *visible* to certain prophets? For example, Moses and the seventy elders *saw* God and ate with Him (see Exod. 24:9-16). To answer this, we must first acknowledge the place called *heaven*, which exists on the outer edge of our universe and is inhabited by the Triune God, ministering spirits and other angels, living creatures, and departed righteous souls.

With the exception of Enoch (Heb. 11:5) and Elijah (2 Kings 2:11), both of whom were transported alive into heaven, righteous men and women who die will leave their bodily remains on the earth. Their soul and spirit is taken to the third heaven, to paradise (2 Cor. 12:4), where they rest and await the resurrection, when Christ returns to raise the righteous dead and gather together the saints living on the earth (1 Thess. 4:16-17).

Paul alluded to the human soul and spirit being separated from the body when he penned, "to be absent from the body is to be present with the Lord" (2 Cor. 5:8). In his *journey to paradise*, Paul said, "whether in the body or out of the body I could not tell" (2 Cor. 12:2). Out of the body refers to his spirit leaving his physical body and traveling to the third heaven and back to earth, which could have occurred fourteen years before he wrote about this experience, when he was stoned in the city of Lystra and left for dead (Acts 14:19). This type of experience is not a vision, but a literal *catching up of the person's spirit* into the region of the third heaven.

There are numerous stories of individuals who experienced a near death or actual death experience and were revived by doctors. They describe leaving the body and traveling deep into the outer cosmos where they saw departed loved ones or the stunning glories of heaven. This supernatural transportation would be considered "out of the body."

Spirit beings—including angels and the spirits of humans—generally are *invisible* to the human eye. At times, angels are present in a room of believers and their presence can be *felt*, but not *seen* in the physical realm. This occurred with Daniel and his Jewish companions, as Daniel *saw* the angelic visitor in minute detail, while the other men saw nothing, but *felt* something (see Dan. 10).

Seeing *nothing* but feeling *something* has been witnessed when people stand at the death bed of a righteous person. Moments before the spirit departs from the body, the dying person may testify to seeing a departed loved one beckoning them to come home, or hovering above them as if preparing for their departure from earth to heaven. I believe the reason for this is that the dying person is, for a brief moment, positioned between two worlds at once: the natural and spiritual, the earthly and heavenly, the visible and invisible. As the believer's eternal soul and spirit prepare to slip out of the body of flesh, the spiritual senses are more alert and instantly become aware of the invisible world they are about to enter. Upon seeing into the celestial world, the dying person will often pass away within moments of expressing what they see.

Doctors often explain these phenomena as imaginative hallucinations caused by chemicals being released in the brain. If this were the case, then every dying person would have these same experiences. However, with respect to the medical community, we cannot expect even the most brilliant researcher to understand or explain strange phenomena that they cannot test in a laboratory or identify under a microscope. When a family surrounds the death bed of a believer, they will seldom see the visiting angels or the spirit of the departed, but they may describe feeling an electrical charge, an unexplained feeling, or a strong peace that enters the room for a brief moment.

When my father's grandmother lay dying, her daughters had gathered around her bed. Moments later she whispered, "Let the nice man in…he's coming for me…let him in." She pointed to the doorway, but the person she saw was invisible to the others in the room. Then she smiled, stretched her hand toward this invisible person, closed her eyes and passed away. Even though they saw nobody, those in the room witnessed a divine holiness that brushed the atmosphere. Dad said that the Christians in the room believed this unseen visitor was likely an angel assigned by the Lord to oversee her transfer from earth to heaven.

There is a reason God does not bring the body to heaven with the soul and spirit (1 Thess. 5:23) at the moment of death. God created the physical body of the first man, Adam, from the dust of the earth; and as noted in Scripture, after death the body gradually deteriorates and returns to the dusty earth from which it came (Gen. 3:19). Scientists say that a human body is composed of certain elements of the earth. Notice the percentage of a few of these elements:

- Carbon – accounts for 18% of body weight

- Calcium – accounts for 1.5% of body weight

- Potassium – accounts for 0.35% of body weight

- Sulfur – accounts for 0.25% of body weight

- Sodium – accounts for 0.15% of body weight

- Magnesium – accounts for 0.05% of body weight

With the exception of the supernatural transportation of Enoch and Elijah to heaven, if the physical body departed from earth's oxygen-filled atmosphere to the third heaven, then *without supernatural intervention*, when traveling beyond the speed of light (186,000 miles per second), the pressure would instantly melt the flesh, disintegrate the bones, and leave nothing but tiny dust particles floating in the vastness of space. At death, the human body remains on earth in a grave, while the spirit and soul are transported into the higher dimension of God's kingdom of light. This is a light realm with so much energy and brightness, that Paul stated "no man can approach (it)" (1 Tim. 6:16), meaning that a mortal man cannot stand in the full manifestation of God's glory.

It is humanly impossible to determine the molecular structure of a spirit, whether angels or the human spirits dwelling within each living human being. In Scripture, both *light* and *fire* are mentioned as components that describe angels when they are visible to humans. For example, the *glory* (seen as light and brightness) that radiates from God is so intense, that when Saul of Tarsus looked into it, he was instantly blinded for three days (Acts 9:3, 9). This brightness is so illuminating that, in the future city of the New Jerusalem, the light from Christ's glory will engulf the entire city and no natural sunlight or artificial light will be required. His light will shine throughout the interior of the fifteen-hundred-square-mile holy metropolis (Rev. 21:23).

The thought of angelic spirits manifesting on earth in the form of *fire* is intriguing, and is recorded throughout the Scripture. When Moses was upon the Mount of God, the glory of God appeared as a *devouring fire* on top of the mountain. There on Mount Sinai, the Law of God was etched upon two stone tablets by the *fiery finger* of God's hand (Exod. 31:18; Deut. 33:2).

Elijah was transported in a whirlwind to heaven, in a chariot engulfed in fire and pulled by fiery spirit horses (2 Kings 2:11). Years later, Elisha awoke one morning, tapped into the invisible world, and saw horses and chariots of fire surrounding a hilltop and protecting him (2 Kings 6:17).

When Ezekiel described God on His throne, he saw Him as "a fire from the loins up and a fire from the loins down" (Ezek. 1:27; 8:2). The Apostle Paul wrote, "Our God is a consuming fire" (Heb. 12:29). In heaven there is a specific angel assigned over the fire on the golden altar where the prayers of all saints ascend before God (Rev. 14:18). From the pillar of fire by night (Exod. 13:21), to the divided tongues as of fire dancing on the heads of the disciples at Pentecost (Acts 2:3-4), the celestial Kingdom of God continually manifests in some form of *fire*.

Scientists tell us that stars in our upper cosmos are hot, burning objects with pockets of both heat and cold. They believe that stars are continually being formed, which should not offend creationists, as the heavens were spoken into being by the Word of God. Since sound waves never die, and since God's Word never passes away (Matt. 24:35), then God's spoken word still echoes throughout the heavens today. Perhaps His command, "Let there be light" still unites the elements necessary to continue expansion of the universe.

In the eyes of the prophets and Biblical visionaries, this fire appears as any normal fire we would see on earth. However, in the world of heavenly spirits, fire must not have the consuming effect that it does in the natural world. Otherwise, everything it touches would either burn or be consumed into ashes or oblivion.

The earth is unique above all stellular spheres, as we have the perfect atmosphere to support life, and we are the perfect distance from the sun to sustain both human and plant life. The earth has a proper mix of life-giving substances, and without this one colorless and odorless gas called oxygen, life would immediately cease on earth. The exact mix of nitrogen and oxygen make up ninety-nine percent of earth's atmosphere. Oxygen has been discovered on other planets; however, those atmospheres are either too hot or too cold, or lack the water necessary to sustain life as we know it.

Nitrogen is not combustible, which is good, because if it were, there might be a combustible explosion every time a match is lit. Oxygen, however, is highly combustible when mixed with certain other gases. For example, liquid oxygen and liquid hydrogen together create rocket fuel.

Fire needs oxygen to burn. Without oxygen, a flame will go out immediately. Now consider what happens when a spirit being, such as an angel, suddenly moves at the speed of light, enters the earth's atmosphere, and makes his invisibility visible. Could the combination of the elements of our atmosphere, when colliding with the spirit body at high speeds, change the structure of that spirit into a fiery form? After all, the Bible speaks of horses and chariots of fire that have manifested in the earthly realm (2 Kings 2). Angels can manifest in three dimensions:

- They can be completely *invisible* to the human eye;

- They can take on the *form of a human being;*

- They can, at times, appear to the human eye in a *fiery form.*

Earth's atmosphere is designed for *physical life* and heaven's atmosphere is designed for *spirit life.* A resurrected human body conceals within it immortal components (a soul and spirit) that are void of any form of death or corruption. Most scholars believe that a resurrected body will require no sleep. When humans sleep at night, the spirit remains active and alert within the body. This explains why a demonic or angelic presence in your bedroom can suddenly awaken you from a sound sleep. The molecular structure of an angelic body, however, must allow it to travel at high velocities from earth to heaven and back, as the heavenly city of God is possibly billions of light years from earth; yet angels can journey across the vastness of space in the blink of an eye. When entering the earth's atmosphere, *it is possible that our atmosphere changes the molecular structure of certain types of spirit beings into beings of fire and intense light.*

The prophet Elisha described horses with the appearance of fire coming to transport Elijah to heaven (2 Kings 2:11; 6:17). However, when the Apostle John saw Christ and His heavenly entourage (armies of heaven) return to earth from heaven at the end of the tribulation, he saw them descend to earth riding white horses (see Rev. 19:14). He did not see horses of fire; they were simply spirit horses that appear similar to our white stallions on earth. Just as the Holy Spirit descended upon Christ in the form of a dove (Matt. 3:16), certain spirits have the ability to transform themselves into different forms.

Since the ethereal world of God is situated in a galaxy that is unknown light years from earth, we are uncertain of the molecular composition of the third heaven where the heavenly spirits dwell, or of how cosmic gases and the elements on earth might be different from those in the highest heaven. Is it possible that, when angelic messengers enter the earth's realm, they can alter their forms from invisible to visible, or take on the form of humans?

Fire is an important Biblical manifestation. At times, a Biblical seer linked God's Divine presence with fire. When Moses saw the burning bush in the desert, we read:

> "And the Angel of the Lord appeared to him in a flame of fire from the midst of a bush. So he looked, and behold, the bush was burning with fire, but the bush was not consumed."
>
> – EXOD. 3:2-3

Manoah, Samson's father, burned an offering on a stone altar to honor God's promise through a heavenly messenger that he and his wife would conceive a son. Suddenly, as the flames burned toward heaven, the angel ascended up to God in the flame of fire from off the altar (Judg. 13:20-21). So we see that it is possible, when an angel enters the earth's atmosphere, for the molecular structure of an angel's body to be altered and appear in human form—a form so detailed that it is difficult to tell whether they are human or angelic. (See also Genesis 19, where the two angels appeared in human form to deliver Lot from Sodom.) God himself manifested at times in the form of fire (Ezek. 1:27).

The temperature of a fire in a fireplace could reach as high as fifteen hundred degrees Fahrenheit, depending on the type of wood and the place where the flame is most intense. The core of the sun is twenty-seven million degrees Fahrenheit, while the sun's surface is about ten million degrees Fahrenheit. When a supernova explosion occurs among the stars, the core temperature reaches nearly eighteen billion degrees Fahrenheit. Countless stars have already burned out and run out of fuel, but because they are millions of light years away, we continue to see their light. With stars, the force of gravity is always pushing at them to collapse them, but nuclear fusion is always pushing out to blow them apart.

THE HEAVENS DESTROYED BY FIRE

The Apostle Peter predicted a complete renovation of the heavens and the earth. At the end of Christ's thousand-year rule on earth, a heavenly judgment involving men and angels is set in heaven. It will be called the great white throne judgment (Rev. 20:11-15). This judgment will seal the doom for all the unrighteous throughout history, including all who died in the tribulation and during the thousand years of Christ's rule (as humans will still be populating the earth at that time). Angels will also receive a final judgment, as the Bible says that saints will serve as the heavenly tribunal to judge the angels (1 Cor. 6:3).

After this judgment, God creates a new heaven and a new earth. This first heaven and earth will be renovated by a massive cosmic fire that will sweep from one end of heaven to the other. The earth's crusty surface will be scorched, as God creates a new, clean earth, free of all disease, sickness, and death. It will be the second creation. Peter saw this when he wrote:

> "But, beloved, do not forget this one thing, that with the Lord one day is as a thousand years, and a thousand years as one day. The Lord is not slack concerning His promise, as some count slackness, but is longsuffering toward us, not willing that any should perish but that all should come to repentance.
>
> But the day of the Lord will come as a thief in the night, in which the heavens will pass away with a great noise, and the elements will melt with fervent heat; both the earth and the works that are in it will be burned up. Therefore, since all these things will be dissolved, what manner of persons ought you to be in holy conduct and godliness, looking for and hastening the coming of the day of God, because of which the heavens will be dissolved, being on fire, and the elements will melt with fervent heat?

Nevertheless we, according to His promise, look for new heavens and a new earth in which righteousness dwells."

– 2 PETER 3:8-13

Thus we see that creation—including heaven and earth—were *born in the fire* and all things will *end in fire.*

GOD—VISIBLE OR INVISIBLE?

Why is God invisible, yet at other times visible? The fact is, He is invisible to human eyes, but is always visible to the spiritual eyes. The New Testament calls God *invisible* in three references (Col. 1:15; 1 Tim. 1:17; Heb. 11:27). Paul noted that God is immortal, invisible and eternal. Those on earth cannot see God's form as He sits on His throne; yet His presence fills every square inch of space in the universe, just like one heat source can warm an entire building.

The emphasis on God being invisible is in the comparison of the true God to idol gods, as in Paul's time, people turned to images they could see. They had little faith in a god they could not touch or look at with their natural eyes. But the Bible tells us, that which is seen is temporal, and that which is not seen is eternal (2 Cor. 4:18).

Prophets have seen God in visions, dreams and trances, and they recorded their revelations in the Holy Bible. It is their revelations that provide us with the information you will learn in this book.

CHAPTER 2

Heaven: Three Levels or Seven?

I N 2 CORINTHIANS 12, the Apostle Paul revealed the existence of a heavenly *paradise* located in what he called the *third heaven* (2 Cor. 12:1-4). Most men identify heaven as the vast space stretching above their heads. However, in many Jewish and Christian writings, the authors speak of numerous levels of heaven, with some suggesting there are seven levels. Are there three levels? Or are there seven? Why is this significant?

The idea of seven heavens is found in numerous religions, including Judaism, Islam, and even early Christianity (including the Roman Catholic Church). This belief of seven levels may have originated among the ancients who knew of seven major heavenly bodies (planets), and in early tradition may have assumed each planet was floating in its own separate heaven.

In the Jewish faith, the number seven is a number of Divine perfection or completion. There are seven days in a week, seven major festivals, and a seven-branched golden menorah that, according to the Jewish historian Josephus, represents the seven planets.

In the Apocalypse, the lamb, a symbol of Christ's sufferings, has seven horns and seven eyes (Rev. 5:6). The number seven is found 463 times throughout the Scripture—more than any other cardinal number.

THE ENOCH REVELATION

Moses, author of the first five books of the Bible (called the Torah), lists the first ten generations of men from Adam to Noah. These individuals, also called antediluvian men (meaning men living before the global flood), lived long lives prior to and shortly after the destructive watery deluge. Among the first ten men, Methuselah, the eighth man listed from Adam, lived the longest at 969 years. The shortest lifespan belonged to Enoch, who lived 365 years before being caught up into heaven (Gen. 5:22-27).

Enoch is perhaps the most unique among the first ten generations. He is considered the first Biblical prophet among the ten, and he is one of the first prophets in human history. Second, his prophetic predictions were the first *on record* to predict the return of the Lord with His saints (see Jude 14). And third, Enoch escaped death by being transported alive into heaven. Moses wrote:

> "Enoch lived sixty-five years, and begot Methuselah. After he begot Methuselah, Enoch walked with God three hundred years, and had sons and daughters. So all the days of Enoch were three hundred and sixty-five years. And Enoch walked with God; and he was not, for God took him."
>
> – GENESIS 5:21-24

Enoch's bodily removal was reiterated in Hebrews 11, where we read:

> "By faith Enoch was taken away so that he did not see death, and was not found, because God had taken him; for before he was taken he had this testimony, that he pleased God."
>
> – HEBREWS 11:5-6

In Biblical types and shadows, the snatching up of Enoch alive into heaven is noted as a "type" of the church being caught up at Christ's coming to meet the Lord in the air (1 Thess. 4:16-17). Centuries later, the prophet Elijah was transported to the celestial world in a whirlwind and a chariot of fire (2 Kings 2).

There is no Biblical account that explains *how* Enoch was snatched up from the earth. Did he simply vanish? One Jewish religious book called *Jashar*—a lesser known manuscript of ancient Jewish history mentioned in Joshua 10:13 and 2 Samuel 1:18—speaks of Enoch's departure:

> "...And it was upon the seventh day that Enoch ascended into heaven in a whirlwind, with horses and chariots of fire..."
>
> *– JASHAR*, III v. 36

If this tradition is correct, then both Enoch and Elijah were taken from the earth in the same manner. I believe that both men will, in the future, return to Jerusalem where they will serve as the two witnesses for forty–two months. At the conclusion of their testimony, both will experience death for the first time, but will be resurrected after three-and-a-half days, and afterward be caught up to heaven at the same time (Rev. 11:7-12). Both men are linked to end-time prophecy, with Malachi predicting that Elijah will reappear before the great tribulation, called the "terrible day of the Lord" (Mal. 4:5).

ANCIENT MANUSCRIPTS AND WRITINGS

As far back as Adam, early mankind spoke a single language—the language Adam spoke when he communicated with God and named the animals (Gen. 2:19). People sometimes question, when did man begin to *write down* the words he was speaking? And in what letter or graphic form was his writing? Did he use word pictures, such as hieroglyphics, or some early form of a lettered alphabet? Are there historical records for evidence of early writing, from Adam to Noah's flood (about 1,656 years)?

In 1767, a scholar named Dr. John Gill believed that Seth, the third son of Adam, was the inventor of an early form of the Hebrew alphabet that was passed to future generations, including Enoch. Books etched in an older form of Hebrew were discovered in Syria and Mesopotamia, and were suggested to be from Seth's writings. Jewish scribes and rabbinical writings (such as the Zohar and the Targum of Jonathan commenting on Genesis 5:24), refer to Enoch as a "great scribe."

Hundreds of years before Christ, the Grecian General Alexander the Great wrote a letter to Aristotle saying:

> "When I came to such a place in *India*, the natives told me that they had with them the sepulcher of an ancient king that ruled over all the world, whose name was *Cainan*, the son of *Enos*, who foreseeing that God would bring a flood upon the earth, wrote his prophecy of it on tables of stone, and they are here; the writing is Hebrew writing."

The Jewish historian Josephus confirmed that these brick and stone pillars existed, and that they had some form of writing that dated back to Seth, who was Cainan's father:

> "They were also inventors of that peculiar sort of wisdom which is concerned with the heavenly bodies and their order. And that their inventions might not be lost before they were sufficiently known, upon Adam's prediction that the world was to be destroyed at one time by the force of fire, and at another time by the violence and quantity of water, they made two pillars; one of brick and the other of stone; they inscribed their discoveries on them both..."
>
> – JOSEPHUS BOOK I, CHAPTER 2, PART 3

This narrative of Seth's son, Cainan, which documented Adam's prediction, is also found in *Jashar*, the sacred book of Jewish history. A book of *Jashar*, written in Hebrew, was discovered and translated into English by a British scholar in 1840. The writer spoke of these same tablets warning of the coming flood:

> "And Cainan knew by his wisdom that God would destroy the sons of men for having sinned upon the earth, and the Lord would in the latter days bring upon them the waters of the flood. And in those days Cainan wrote upon tablets of stone, what was to take place at the time to come and put them in his treasury."
>
> – JASHAR II, VERSES 12-13

Prior to and during the time of the early church in the first century A.D., a series of writings was identified as the Book of Enoch.

A passage from the book of Enoch is quoted by Jude in the New Testament, where we read:

> "Now Enoch, the seventh from Adam, prophesied about these men also, saying, "Behold, the Lord comes with ten thousands of His saints, to execute judgment on all, to convict all who are ungodly among them of all their ungodly deeds which they have committed in an ungodly way, and of all the harsh things which ungodly sinners have spoken against Him."

> – JUDE 14-15

This statement is credited to a paragraph in the book of Enoch, which was known and quoted in the early church by such fathers as Clement and Irenaeus, and is also in the writings of Barnabas. Numerous quotes from Enoch are often used when connecting the mystery of fallen angels and the origin of the race of giants on the earth (Gen 6:1-4).

Clement (A.D. 30-100), the bishop of Rome and personal friend of the Apostle Paul, wrote that Enoch never died:

> "Let us take (for instance) Enoch, who, being found righteous in obedience, was translated, and death was never known to happen to him" (*First Epistle of Clement to the Corinthians*, chapter 9).

Barnabas (A.D. 44), who accompanied the Apostle Paul on his first missionary journey, referred to the prophecies of Enoch, who said:

> "For this end the Lord has cut short the times and the days, that His Beloved may hasten; and He will come to the inheritance" *(Epistle of Barnabas, chapter 4).*

Irenaeus (A.D. 180) published his work, *Against Heresies,* in which he spoke of Enoch, whose translation was a prophetic view of our future rapture:

> "For Enoch, when he pleased God, was translated in the same body in which he did please Him, thus pointing out by anticipation the translation of the just" *(Against Heresies,* bk. 5).

The idea that Enoch recorded information that was later recopied and handed down is also a belief among some Jewish rabbis. Some even suggest that Enoch's writings were taken aboard the ark with Noah, and are some of the oldest writings passed down in the world.

In the 1950s, fragments of the book of Enoch were discovered in the Qumran caves near the Dead Sea. Critics say the book was never written by Enoch, and was a fraud compiled much later. However, there are numerous references to the writings of Enoch in the volumes of writings by early church fathers, especially on the subject of fallen angels.

THE REDISCOVERY OF THE BOOK

In 1733, a traveler named Bruce James obtained three copies of the book of Enoch and brought them to Europe, where it was translated into several European languages and eventually into English. Later, a Greek translation surfaced that matched the Coptic translation. A Professor Laurence (Archbishop of Cashel) published the first English version in 1821 and again in 1833.

When comparing the 1611 English translation of Jude 14 from the Greek text, with an early translation from the book of Enoch itself, we read:

> "Now Enoch, the seventh from Adam, prophesied about these men also, saying, "Behold, the Lord comes with ten thousands of His saints, to execute judgment on all, to convict all who are ungodly among them of all their ungodly deeds which they have committed in an ungodly way, and of all the harsh things which ungodly sinners have spoken against Him."
>
> – JUDE 14-15

The same verse below is translated to English from the book of Enoch, and it reads:

> "And behold, he comes with myriads of the holy to pass judgment upon them, and will destroy the impious, and will call to account all flesh for everything the sinners and the impious have done and committed against him"
>
> – ENOCH 1:9

In the first nine verses from the book of Enoch, interesting insight is recorded:

"The words of the blessing of Enoch wherewith he blessed the chosen and just, who will exist on the day of tribulation when all the wicked and impious shall be removed.

"And then answered and spoke Enoch, a just man, whose eyes were opened by God so that he saw a holy vision in the heavens, which the angels showed to me, and from them I heard everything, and I knew what I saw, but not for this generation, but for the far-off generations, which are to come.

"Concerning the chosen I spoke and conversed concerning them with the Holy and Great One, who will come from his abode, the God of the world. And from there he will step on to Mount Sinai, and appear with his hosts, and appear in the strength of his power from heaven.

"And all will fear, and the watchers will tremble, and great fear and terror will seize them to the ends of the earth. And the exalted mountains will be shaken, and the high hills will be lowered, and will melt like wax before the flame.

"And the earth will be submerged, and everything that is on the earth will be destroyed, and there will be a judgment upon everything, and upon all the just.

"But to the just he will give peace, and will protect the chosen, and mercy will abide over them, and they will all be God's, and will be prosperous and blessed, and the light of God will shine for them.

"And behold, he comes with myriads of the holy to pass judgment upon them, and will destroy the impious, and will call to account all flesh for everything the sinners and the impious have done and committed against him"

– ENOCH 1:1-9

Notice the vision was for far-off (future) generations. The writer compares the return of the Lord to God coming down on Mount Sinai with a host of His angels, at the giving of the Law, which is recorded in Exodus 19. In this Exodus narrative, there was thunder, lightning, and the voice of a trumpet sounding loud and long. In Exodus 19, the *Lord came down* and *Moses went up* (Exod. 19:20). A careful rendering of the events on Mount Sinai paints the imagery of the catching away of the righteous at the return of Christ (1 Thess. 4:16-17). The Enoch prediction indicates that, at the time of the end, *terror* will grip the world as the entire planet will be shaken. He then moves forward to the time when the Lord returns with myriads of the holy.

Interestingly, all of these predictions and events can be traced throughout both the Old and New Testament. The book of Enoch also speaks of different levels of heaven.

The theory of seven levels of heaven is based upon a tradition stating that Enoch was asleep and weeping in a dream, when two very tall men appeared to him. They had the appearance of angels, with gold wings, eyes like burning lamps, and faces bright as the sun. The two men awoke Enoch and beckoned him to journey with them into heaven.

Being carried on the angels' wings, Enoch ascended to the first heaven where he observed the treasuries of ice, snow, clouds and dew, and two hundred angels assigned to these elements in the first heaven.

In the second heaven, Enoch allegedly saw fallen angels imprisoned who had disobeyed God. In the level of the third heaven, he was shown Paradise, fruit trees, flowers, and delightful fragrances. There he saw the tree of life, described as gold and crimson in appearance and as transparent as fire. Four streams were said to flow from the roots of the tree. He is said to have seen three hundred angels who keep the garden of Paradise. (Ginsburg; *Legends of the Jews*)

Without continuing further, while Enoch was the first Biblical prophet who knew a flood was coming, and who saw the return of the Lord to earth and the judgment against the ungodly, some of the accounts of his ascension into the heavens seem embellished. Parts of the narrative are contrary to both modern science and certain Scriptures. Yet, there are levels of heaven according to the Divine revelation of the Bible.

THE LEVELS OF HEAVEN

In the Old Testament, the word heavens (plural) is used frequently, implying there is a division of the heavens into different spheres or levels. The only Scripture that specifies an exact number of levels is in 2 Corinthians 12:2-4, where Paul spoke of being caught up into the third heaven. This can be easily understood, as we recognize the earth's atmosphere as the first heaven; the cosmic heavens of the sun, moon and stars as the second heaven; and the unseen regions beyond the stars as the third heaven. The question I always asked was: What is beyond the third heaven, other than just endless space?

From the Biblical perspective, there are three distinct heavens. The first is the dominion given to man. The second is given to angels, including Satan's spirit rebels (Eph. 6:12). The third, being under complete control of God Himself, is His eternal dwelling place.

The number *three* is important, as it is a Biblical number representing *unity*. Notice some of the threes in the Bible:

- The Father, the Word, and the Holy Spirit (1 John 5:7)

- Chief angels Michael, Gabriel, Lucifer (Jude 9; Luke 1:19; Isa. 14:12)

- Body, soul, and spirit (1 Thess. 5:23)

- Faith, hope, and love (1 Cor. 13:13)

- Sun, moon, and stars (Gen. 37:9)

- The temple chambers: outer court, inner court, and Holy of Holies (Exod. 26)

- The contents of the Ark: manna, rod of Aaron, and tables of the Covenant (Heb. 9:4)

- Three branches on each side, and three bowls on each branch of the golden menorah (Exod. 25:32-33)

31

- Three in Christ's inner circle: Peter, James, and John (Matt. 17:1)

- Three vocal gifts: tongues, interpretation, and prophecy (1 Cor. 12:7-10)

- Three mind gifts: wisdom, knowledge, and faith (1 Cor. 12:7-10)

- Three power gifts: healing, miracles, and discerning of spirits (1 Cor. 12:7-10)

The first heaven, man's dominion, has the air we breathe. It is where planes fly and birds soar. The second heaven begins above the outer atmosphere and extends through an unknown number of miles into outer space. It includes the cosmic lights and stretches far beyond where powerful manmade telescopes can see. Somewhere at the edge of the galaxy, an invisible line is crossed as the atmosphere changes and the glory of God permeates the outer layer. This is the land of heaven, and the region identified as the third heaven.

When God created man, Satan had already been expelled from the third heaven to the second heaven. Then Adam sinned and released his dominion to Satan. After Christ defeated Satan, the church was given spiritual dominion on earth over demons and evil spirits (Luke 10:19), and Satan remained in the upper cosmos and became the "accuser of the brethren" (Rev. 12:10). After the saints are caught up to meet Christ in the air and are received in the heavenly temple, this accuser is then violently cast down to earth by Michael the archangel (Rev. 12:7-10). At that moment there is great rejoicing in heaven (Rev. 12:12) as the words of the accuser are heard no more in the heavenly temple!

If there are three heavens, and the final and third heaven is the land of eternal life, then what is beyond this heaven? That was the question I asked myself while lying in bed, looking out the window at the silver stars shooting their radiance back in my direction.

Is there only empty darkness with no light? Are there no colorful gases and nebulas? Do the light and glory end at the third heaven? There is no definitive answer to this question. We may never know until we arrive in heaven where all of our questions will be answered. However, since God dwells in the third heaven, that is the one we should be interested in and the one we should set our affections upon.

CHAPTER 3

Sapphires: God's Favorite Gemstone

Y EARS AGO, I was intrigued when I read a Jewish tradition about the type of stone upon which the first set of the Ten Commandments was written. Jewish sages teach that the original Ten Commandment stones were engraved by the hand of God on two sapphire stones:

> "Ancient Jewish scholars state that the sapphire employed for the tables was taken from the throne of glory" *(Legends of the Jews,* by Ginzberg, Volume 6, page 49).

According to the Jewish Midrash, the tablets of stone were made of blue sapphire as a symbol of the heavens and God's throne, and were written by the *finger of God* (Exod. 31:18). The Hebrew letters were said to be bored fully through the stone (Ex. 32:15), which was a miracle, since the inner markings of some of the Hebrew letters (such as samekh and the final mem) floated in place. Moreover, even though the letters were bored fully through the stone, both sides appeared normally; that is, the back of the tablet looked identical to the front (Source: *The Midrash* - Shabbos 104a).

This beautiful tradition of these two stones being sapphire is scientifically possible when you understand how a sapphire stone is created in the earth. The sapphire is the second hardest mineral known to man. It requires aluminum oxide, along with volcanic heat and pressure to eventually form sapphires. When liquid magma deep within the earth cools, the minerals dissolve, cool, and form crystals. As the aluminum oxide cools, the mineral impurities that seep into the crystals begin to create beautiful colors. Titanium and iron also assist in the formation of the blue sapphire. It takes pressure and *intense heat* to form the necessary crystals that eventually produce the sapphire.

Moses reported that, when he received the law of God on Mount Sinai, the Lord Himself wrote upon the tables of stone with his finger—a finger of fire (Deut. 9:10). Since a percentage of the earth's crust contains aluminum oxide, when the fire from God's hand burnt letters into the surface of the rock, the intense heat theoretically could have turned the oxides and minerals within the stones into a crystal form, creating a set of sapphire stones that Moses carried off the mountain.

What secular scientists claim would take millions of years to form under the fire and pressure of the earth, could have been created immediately by the finger of God, in the same manner that Christ turned water into wine in mere seconds (John 2:1-10).

The color *blue* is also important in the Jewish religion, as blue has always represented heaven, as far back as the construction of the Tabernacle. Curtains of blue are mentioned forty-four times in Exodus alone.

In the Law, Jewish men were required to place tassels on the four corner of their garments, and insert a permanent blue thread in all four corners of the prayer shawl (Num. 15:38). The tassel and the blue thread were a reminder to remember God's Commandments that He gave to Israel (Num. 15:39).

This heavenly blue was the color God selected for the robe of the ephod of the High Priest, as his robe was "all of blue." Sewn on the hem of the priestly garment were woven pomegranates of blue, purple and scarlet (Exod. 28:31). *The deep, rich blue color of expensive sapphires is a reminder of the upper region of the supernal heaven.*

DAD'S REMARKABLE EXPERIENCE

When my father, Fred Stone, was in his late teens, the Korean War broke out and the draft board was interviewing young men from the rural communities in West Virginia. These young men were raised to be expert hunters, and many were already superior marksmen. Dad was in prayer concerning his call into the ministry and was considering going into the war as a chaplain or a medical assistant.

He went to a small, one-room cabin to study and to pray for God's will in His life. While sitting outside in a cane-back chair with his Bible on his lap, he felt a hand reach through the wall and touch him. Suddenly, he felt his body slump over, and immediately he was outside his physical body, looking back at himself slumped over. He thought he must have had a heart attack and died.

Dad described how his spirit came out of his body, like removing a hand from a glove. Within seconds he was moving with great speed into the upper atmosphere and out into the cosmos. The pressure was so intense that his eyes were shut, and his spirit was in a fetal position. He thought that he was being pulled toward the highest heaven, or God's eternal dwelling.

Suddenly he felt himself stop and when he looked, he was standing on nothing—no floor, no ground, nothing. He was suspended in space, completely surrounded by what he called a *sapphire blue heaven*. All around, over and under, to the left and the right, was the same shade of rich, sapphire blue.

Without going into further detail, Dad was given a Divine mandate to enter the ministry full-time. His spirit returned to earth and reentered his body. His hair was standing straight up and his body was shaking all over. He was filled with a combination of awe, reverence, and trembling for quite some time. The draft board in Beckley, West Virginia told Dad that if they needed him they would contact him. They never did.

The point I wish to make is the appearance of the sapphire-colored heaven. This seems to be the color of the atmosphere in heaven, and in the upper regions beyond the planet of heaven. There is no sun, moon or stars; just a royal, sapphire blue atmosphere that extends beyond the beyond.

THE COLORS OF THE THRONE

When Solomon was preparing the Temple in Jerusalem, we read an unusual verse:

> "And refined gold by weight for the altar of incense, and for the construction of the chariot, that is, the gold cherubim that spread their wings and overshadowed the ark of the covenant of the Lord."
>
> — 1 CHRONICLES 28:18 (NKJV)

The Hebrew word for *chariot* here is *merkabah*. Jewish mystics call the Divine vision penned in Ezekiel chapter one, *the Mystery of the Merkabah*, meaning that when God's throne is carried by four mighty angels, it becomes God's traveling chariot. It is a word found in Ezekiel's writings. In Ezekiel chapters one and ten, the visionary prophet sees the *spirit* that releases the life-force into the cherubim. He writes about wheels within wheels that are covered with eyes, and that are spinning and releasing Divine energy (Ezekiel 1:15-20). The Biblical imagery indicates that God's throne is positioned in the heavenly temple. However, at specific times, specially assigned cherubim (angels) raise God's throne and can transport it through the heavens to earth on their wings (Ezek. 10:1).

The writer of Chronicles alludes to the Ark of the Covenant and the two gold cherub on the Mercy Seat (the gold lid covering the Ark), and calls it the *chariot* (1 Chron. 28:18). The Hebrew word for *chariot* in 1 Chronicles 28:18 is also *merkabah*, which is the same word used by rabbis to identify the throne of God when it is being carried by the cherubim. Thus both the Ark (the golden chariot) and the throne (God's sapphire chariot) can both be lifted and carried. The sacred rectangular gold box was carried on the shoulders of four priests, using long wooden poles covered with gold that slipped into gold rings on the bottom sides of the Ark of the Covenant. These poles carrying the Ark rested upon the shoulders of four priestly Levites to prevent them from touching the Ark itself.

THE ARK AS A CAPACITOR

A capacitor is an electrical component that stores energy electrostatically. Years ago in Israel, Tom Evenson, a friend from Lenoir City, Tennessee, was with our tour group in Jerusalem when we visited the Temple Institute and Museum—designed to teach visitors about the Jewish temple. The beautiful white stone building housed numerous models, including a miniature replica of the Ark of the Covenant.

The Institute guide pointed out that, according to their Jewish sources, the Ark of the Covenant actually consisted of three individual boxes that fit together as one. The outer box was rectangular wood covered within and without with gold. The middle box was all wood, and the third box was made of thin, 24-karat gold that lay within the wooden box. When Tom, an electrician, saw how the three separate boxes were placed together, he spoke up and said, "This is a natural capacitor for electricity!"

He further explained, "There is static electricity in the air, and this is why you can walk on carpet and touch someone or something and receive a slight shock. The way this Ark is constructed, it will collect and build up the electricity in the air. If you were to touch it with one hand, you would get a terrible shock. But with both hands, under certain conditions, it could electrocute you."

I asked, "How could the priests carry it without harm?"

Tom replied, "The staves would ground out any electricity, so the key was in the wooden poles."

Upon hearing Tom's explanation, the guide said, "Uzzah touched the Ark with both hands and he died" (see 2 Sam. 6:3-8).

While we as believers know this was God's supernatural judgment, the woman was impressed with the natural explanation of how the electrical energy could build up around the Ark and send a death shock into Uzzah.

The Ark was a miniature throne of God upon the earth. The imagery of four priests carrying the Ark is parallel to the four cherubim assigned to lift the throne up and transport the chariot of God from place to place. Four priests were needed for the Ark; and four cherubim, with the faces of a man, ox, lion and eagle, bear up God's throne (Ezek. 1:5-10).

The power of the Ark was witnessed when Israel seized possession of the Promised Land; witness the Jordan River drying up and the walls of Jericho falling (Josh. 3:11-17; 6:4-20). When the Ark went before the people, it was as though God Himself was preparing the way for them.

The Ark was the central piece of sacred furniture when Joshua divided the tribes—six on mount Ebal and six on Mount Gerizim—and pronounced the blessing and curse of the law upon the tribes (Josh. 8:30-35). When the Ark was in Israel's possession, the belief was that God's favor rested upon their endeavors. This blessing ceased when the Ark was captured by Israel's enemies, as then the "glory of God had departed from Israel" (1 Sam. 4:21-22).

As king of Israel, David brought the Ark from Moses' Tabernacle and housed the golden box in a tent the king had prepared, where continual worship was assigned to singers, musicians and scribes, who recorded the many inspired and prophetic utterances from within the tent (1 Chron. 15; 16:1). During his later years, David had prepared detailed plans to construct a Temple to God, but because he was a man of war and not peace, he was unable to fulfill his desire (1 Chron. 28:3). These amazing plans were passed down to David's son, Solomon. King Solomon patterned the Temple in Jerusalem after the Divine pattern of God's eternal throne room in heaven—the pattern of the chariot of the cherubim (2 Chron. 28:18).

As Solomon initiated his construction plan, he built a throne of ivory and overlaid the seat with pure gold. At the rear above the throne was a circular canopy. The throne sat above the people and required six steps to ascend and reach the seat of the king. The golden seat had a left and right armrest with two (carved) lions on either side. Lions were common symbols of royalty in the east; however, the lion was also an emblem of Judah, Solomon's tribal family. There were twelve total carved lions—six on both the left and the right steps—representing the twelve tribes of Israel (1 Kings 10:18-20).

The Old Testament prophets were familiar with the *thrones of kings*.

This may be why, when the Biblical prophets experienced visions of heaven and of God sitting upon His throne, they all emphasized different parts of their view within their visions. Listed below are eight references by five Biblical writers of their throne room experience.

"Then Micaiah said, "Therefore hear the word of the Lord: I saw the Lord sitting on His throne, and all the host of heaven standing on His right hand and His left."

– 2 CHRON. 18:18

"In the year that King Uzziah died, I saw the Lord sitting on a throne, high and lifted up, and the train of His robe filled the temple. Above it stood seraphim; each one had six wings: with two he covered his face, with two he covered his feet, and with two he flew. And one cried to another and said: "Holy, holy, holy is the Lord of hosts; the whole earth is full of His glory! And the posts of the door were shaken by the voice of him who cried out, and the house was filled with smoke."

– ISAIAH 6:1-4 (NKJV)

"And above the firmament over their heads was the likeness of a throne, in appearance like a sapphire stone; on the likeness of the throne was a likeness with the appearance of a man high above it. Also from the appearance of His waist and upward I saw, as it were, the color of amber with the appearance of fire all around within it; and from the appearance of His waist and downward I saw, as it were, the appearance of fire with brightness all around. Like the appearance of a rainbow in a cloud on a rainy day, so was the appearance of the brightness all around it. This was the appearance of the likeness of the glory of the Lord."

– EZEKIEL 1:26-28 (NKJV)

"And I looked, and there in the firmament that was above the head of the cherubim, there appeared something like a sapphire stone, having the appearance of the likeness of a throne."

– EZEKIEL 10:1-2 (NKJV)

"I watched till thrones were put in place,
And the Ancient of Days was seated;
His garment was white as snow,
And the hair of His head was like pure wool.

His throne was a fiery flame,
Its wheels a burning fire;
A fiery stream issued
And came forth from before Him.
A thousand thousands ministered to Him;
Ten thousand times ten thousand stood before Him.
The court was seated,
And the books were opened.

– DANIEL 7:9-10 (NJKV)

"Immediately I was in the Spirit; and behold, a throne set in heaven, and One sat on the throne. And He who sat there was like a jasper and a sardius stone in appearance; and there was a rainbow around the throne, in appearance like an emerald. Around the throne were twenty-four thrones, and on the thrones I saw twenty-four elders sitting, clothed in white robes; and they had crowns of gold on their heads. And from the throne proceeded lightnings, thunderings, and voices. Seven lamps of fire were burning before the throne, which are the seven Spirits of God. Before the throne there was a sea of glass, like crystal. And in the midst of the throne, and around the throne, were four living creatures full of eyes in front and in back."

– REVELATION 4:2-6 (NKJV)

"And I saw in the right hand of Him who sat on the throne a scroll written inside and on the back, sealed with seven seals."

– REVELATION 5:1 (NKJV)

"Then I saw a great white throne and Him who sat on it, from whose face the earth and the heaven fled away. And there was found no place for them. And I saw the dead, small and great, standing before God, and books were opened. And another book was opened, which is the Book of Life..."

– REVELATION 20:11-12 (NKJV)

"And he showed me a pure river of water of life, clear as crystal, proceeding out of the throne of God and of the Lamb."

– REVELATION 22:1 (NKJV)

"The Lord is in His holy temple, the Lord's throne is in heaven."

– PSALM 11:4 (NKJV)

Each visionary saw the throne of God in heaven, although none gave an estimated size of the throne itself. When seeing the Lord, He is described with the *appearance* of man (Ezek. 1:26). Since man was created in the "image" of God (Gen. 1:26), our physical frame consists of hands, legs, eyes, a mouth and so forth; all which are attributes of God Himself. The Almighty is not a cosmic blob of glowing white glory, feeding off the hydrogen and nitrogen in the terrestrial world. According to Scriptures, the Almighty has the appearance similar to His most valued creation, man.

The size of God Himself is never revealed, although His presence can be in all places (Psalms 139:7-12). The outward appearance of God is described as a *jasper* and as a *sardine* stone (Rev. 4:3). The jasper can be found in a variety of colors, but the primary colors are yellows and reds. The red jasper was a royal stone worn by princes or royalty in ancient times. The sardine is also a blood-red colored gemstone. These stones identify the kingship and Divine rule of God over His creation. This red can be compared to the hot flame in a burning fire.

Daniel saw God arrayed in a white garment with hair *white* like wool (Dan. 7:9). Ezekiel also described the appearance of God as the color of *amber* (Ezek. 1:26-27), which is a clear, yellowish stone. When Isaiah saw the Lord, He was sitting on His throne and His train (the outer flowing extension of his robe) filled the heavenly Temple (Isa. 6:1-4). The prophets observed a large heavenly host (a word actually meaning armies) of angels positioned at attention on the left and right side of God's throne (2 Chron. 18:18) with multitudes of saints surrounding the throne and worshipping the Almighty (Dan. 7:9-10), along with twenty-four elders on thrones, combined with unique, four-faced living creatures (Rev. 4:2-8).

God's throne is described with two different colors and appearances. At the final judgment of humanity, God is seated upon a great *white* throne, indicating He is the *righteous* judge, as the color white (for example, white linen, Rev. 19:14) represents righteousness. David wrote, "But the Lord shall endure forever; He has prepared His throne for judgment" (Ps. 9:7).

Ezekiel, however, saw the Lord sitting upon a throne made from a sapphire (blue) stone (Ezek. 1:26). The sapphire color and sapphire stone also manifested when God descended upon the mountain to eat with Moses and the seventy elders. We read:

> "And they saw the God of Israel. And there was under His feet as it were a paved work of sapphire stone, and it was like the very heavens in its clarity."
>
> – EXODUS 24:10

The text indicates that Moses, Aaron, Nadab and Abihu, along with seventy elders, saw God and ate a covenant meal on the top of the mountain. Afterwards, God instructed Moses to come up onto the mountain to receive the commandment stones. Because the place on the mountain where God walked became a sapphire stone, and because the throne of the Lord appears to be a sapphire stone, this is also a part of the *Jewish tradition* that God actually took a section from His sapphire throne to write the Ten Commandments.

Over four hundred years before the Exodus, God made an eternal covenant with Abraham that He would bless his future son and form from his descendants a mighty nation that would bless all nations of the world. The Bible says, "For when God made a promise to Abraham, because He could swear by no one greater, He swore by Himself" (Heb. 6:13-14). When God makes an oath and swears by Himself, He is literally confirming the oath using His own throne because God's Word and throne are everlasting:

> "You, O Lord, remain forever; your throne from generation to generation."
>
> – LAMENTATIONS 5:19

THE CRYSTAL FIRMAMENT

Here on earth, there is an upper stratosphere circling the planet that forms a canopy. From earth's view, the sky is a light blue color on a clear day, and becomes black as the sun sets and night closes in. This is part of God's original law of light and darkness, day and night (Gen.

1:5, 18). However, the atmosphere of heaven above God's throne is described by Ezekiel:

> "The likeness of the firmament above the heads of the living creatures was like the color of an awesome crystal, stretched out over their heads."
>
> — Ezekiel 1:22 (NKJV)

The Amplified reads:

> "Over the head of the [combined] living creature there was the likeness of a firmament, looking like the terrible and awesome [dazzling or shining] crystal or ice stretched across the expanse of sky over their heads."
>
> — Ezekiel 1:22

Depending upon the weather, the earth's atmosphere is covered, at times with white, grey or black clouds. In the upper regions of heaven (third heaven), where the sapphire throne of God sits, there is above God's throne the appearance of an awesome crystal. The word crystal is used twice in the English translation of the Old Testament, and in one Biblical translation means a form of transparent glass (Job 28:17). The *crystal* in the Ezekiel passage is the Hebrew word *qerach*, and it refers to *ice*. It can also allude to *hail* and is translated as ice and frost in the KJV. When light strikes certain ice formations, at different angles, it can create reflections of blue, green, orange and yellow—the color of a prism.

Years ago I recall seeing one of the most beautiful scenes imaginable. It was late December, and Pam and I were returning from my grandparents' home in Davis, West Virginia. It had rained the night before, and the cold air had frozen all the trees in layers of ice and icicles. As the light from the morning sun struck the trees, the ice began to shimmer, making the trees appear to be covered in sheets of diamonds. It was so striking that I thought: What on earth could be more beautiful than this? It was truly a winter wonderland. Years later, I read of this crystal ice firmament and imagined what the skyline or heavenly atmosphere looks like when the light of God radiates in the atmosphere of heaven.

Ezekiel was *on earth as he looked up* and saw the massive crystal-like firmament above his head moving toward the earth. John, on the other hand, is *in heaven* looking down toward the earth through a massive floor of God's Temple, which he describes: *"Before the throne there was a sea of glass like a crystal"* (Rev. 4:6). The word *sea* in this passage is the same Greek word used to describe the sea as a large body of water. When a sea is calm, the light from the sun can cause an almost blinding reflection off the surface of the water.

John saw a floor and Ezekiel saw an upper heavenly atmosphere. One is like ice in appearance and John's (in the Greek) is like a crystal rock, perhaps similar to a diamond. Throughout the book of Revelation, John stood on the crystal floor and observed the transparent floor change colors. He named it the *sea of glass*, and described it first as a crystal in Rev. 4:6. Later, when the 144,000 Jewish men arrive out of the tribulation, John saw this multitude standing on the sea of glass and the crystal floor appeared to be "mingled with fire" (Rev. 15:2). In the throne room, the colors reflecting on the crystal floor change depending upon the type of light being manifest and the angel or person involved in the imagery.

SOMETHING COMING FROM THE THRONE

In John's apocalyptic vision, there are *three unusual sounds* proceeding out of the throne of God:

> *"And out of the throne proceeded lightning and thunder and voices: and there were seven lamps of fire burning before the throne, which are the seven Spirits of God."*
>
> - REV. 4:5 (NKJV)

In the Old Testament it was common, especially when Moses was on Mount Sinai, for the audible voice of the Lord to manifest in a form that sounded like *thunder.* When we hear thunder, it can explode in the atmosphere in a very deep, booming and rumbling sound, and can often be so powerful that it shakes a building. Thunder is caused by (and follows) lightning, as light travels faster than sound. The closer the lightning, the sooner thunder is heard.

When the Lord descended upon Mount Sinai, there were flashes of lightning and pounding thunder (Exod. 20:18). Job wrote, *"Have you an arm like God? Or can you thunder with a voice like His* (Job 40:9)? The psalmist said, *"The voice of your thunder was in the whirlwind; the lightnings lit up the world; the earth trembled and shook* (Psa. 77:18).

God spoke to Christ out of heaven and we read, "Therefore the people who stood by and heard it said that it had thundered." Others said, "An angel has spoken to Him" (John 12:29). The thunder in the book of Revelation that is coming out of the throne is symbolic of the *voice of God* Himself, speaking from His throne in His heavenly temple.

The manifestation of lightning has always, even among the ancients, represented *God's power.* It also represents the speed in which angels are sent traveling throughout the galaxy from heaven to earth. When the cherubim were seen carrying God's sapphire throne from the northern heavens, Ezekiel wrote that they run and return like a flash of lightning (Ezek. 1:14). Since lightning moves at the speed of light—about 186,000 miles per second—and since the earth's equator is 25,000 miles in circumference, this means that after entering earth's atmosphere, an angel that travels the speed of light can circle the equator over seven times in just one second.

The prophet Habbakuk wrote:

> "His brightness was like the light; He had rays flashing from His hand, and there His power was hidden."
>
> – HABBABUK 3:4

The most unusual sound to emit from the throne is simply called *voices*—not a single voice or the sound of one mighty voice, as heard throughout the book of Revelation when John said, "I heard the voice of....the trumpet, seven thunders, seven angels, and great voices of a multitude..." (Rev. 8:13; 10:3, 4; 11:15). Coming out of the throne are unexplained sounds of many *voices* (Rev. 11:19; 16:18). Who or what are these voices?

The *prayers and praise* of the saints on earth instantly make their way to God's heavenly temple; so we must ask, what happens to your words once they leave your mouth? Do they just go into the atmosphere and eventually waft their way upward into the ears of the Almighty over days, weeks or months?

In the time of Jerusalem's Jewish temple, silver and gold vessels were used to hold sacred oil for lighting the menorah, and for ointments, incense and other items needed for the daily priestly rituals. This included silver vessels for catching the blood of the sacrifices and pouring out the blood at the base of the brass altar. Twice a day the High Priest would offer incense on the golden altar, as the people believed that the words of the prayers of all the righteous who prayed facing Jerusalem would hover in the Holy Place and, as the smoke ascended from the burning incense, their words would be transported upward, directly into the heavenly temple (Psalms 141:2).

Scripture tells us that around God's throne are twenty-four thrones with elders seated upon the thrones. These men are believed by many scholars to be the twelve sons of Jacob from the Old Testament and the twelve apostles of Christ from the New Testament, totaling twenty-four. In their hands are golden vials full of the prayers of the saints (Rev. 5:8).

Thus our prayers are reserved in heaven until the moment they are released from the golden vials to be answered. Some prayers are answered immediately and others can be delayed for various reasons.

Then there are the *praises* of God's people. Just as prayer is words, our praise is also words; both are directed upward to God. Nowhere does Scripture indicate that our *praise and worship* is stored up in a golden bowl or in any other specific location. If the motive and heart are pure, praise is received immediately before the throne of God in heaven.

Since our words can justify us or condemn us (Matt. 12:37), and since we will give an account at the judgment seat of Christ of both deeds and words spoken on earth (Rom. 14:11-12; 1 Pet. 4:5), our words have eternal weight. This means words of prayer and praise are significant to God in heaven.

The psalmist wrote, "But You are holy, enthroned in the praises of Israel" (Psa. 22:3). Years ago I talked to a missionary who worked in various Asian nations. He said that one of their Bibles translated this verse, "God sits on His throne, riding on the praises of His people." In light of this interpretation, the voices coming from within the throne could be the countless praises from God's people that exalt the Almighty as He is "high and lifted up on His throne." God is called the Most High, or the lofty one (Isa. 57:15) as he dwells high above all levels of the cosmic heaven, sits in the highest heaven, on the highest throne, above all principalities and powers in heavenly places (Eph. 1:20-21). Out of the sapphire throne pours the words of praise from the inhabitants on earth.

Sapphire is perhaps the darkest blue stone among the spectrum of all gemstones. Since blue is the color identified with heaven, the sapphire throne of God reflects God as the God of heaven. God is known as the God of Abraham (Gen. 31:53), identifying Him with His covenant to Abraham. He is God of the spirits of all flesh (Num. 27:16), revealing Him as the creator of all mankind. As the God of Israel (1 Sam. 1:17), He is the guardian of His chosen people. As the God of salvation, He is able to deliver mankind (Psa. 25:5). He is also called the God of heaven (Neh. 2:20). As the God of heaven, He sits far above and beyond the earthly and imaginative idols of men. Being God of heaven, the color blue is linked with His heavenly position and authority. Thus He is surrounded with blue and sits on a throne of sapphire.

With the many references to sapphire and God's presence, there is something about a sapphire that could make one believe it just might be His favorite stone.

CHAPTER 4

Sons of God and the Morning Stars

IN CONTEMPORARY SOCIETY, much of what we mentally visualize related to the spirit world is seeded in the mind by animation, imaginative writers, and makeup artists in the movie industry. On the big screen, a demonic entity might be portrayed with bleached, wiry hair, greyish skin with fish-like scales, miniature horns growing from his head, gnarled brown teeth, and blood red eyes. Add long, curved, sharp fingernails and a hunchback, and you have a Hollywood masterpiece, designed to frighten theater goers.

Then there is Satan himself. As a child, I recall the printed images of "old splitfoot," as the old timers called him. Of course, since he was the prince of hell, his skin was always red. He sported a fiery red goatee and two goat horns protruding from his head. Artists drew him with a long red tail, tipped with a sharp point. He held a pitchfork in one hand, as though waiting to pierce an unsuspecting victim and roast him over an open flame in hell's pit. If I were to ask a hundred secular people what Satan looks like, many would identify him with the above imagery.

As movies have become more computer-animated, the depictions of Satan and evil spirits have become more complex and frightening. What most biblically uninformed people do not know is that Satan likely looks nothing like the images on the screen or the drawings of imaginative artists. He was and continues to be an angel—a fallen angel, but an angel nonetheless—and was once noted for his beauty, not his frightening appearance.

SATAN—A CREATED ANGEL

In heaven, God created angels with various characteristics and different features. The one classification of angels alluded to more in Scripture than any other is the cherub. The word cherub (the singular form of the word) is mentioned thirty times in twenty-one verses in the Bible—all in the Old Testament. Cherubim (the plural form of the word), is mentioned sixty-five times in fifty-seven verses, all in the Old Testament, except for Hebrews 9:5, a passage referring to the cherubim that overshadow the mercy seat on the Ark of the Covenant.

Satan was created by God at the very beginning of creation. The prophet Ezekiel informed his readers that there was an anointed cherub, whom we can identify as the fallen angel, Satan. The first anointed cherub (Satan) was created with pipes and tabrets, which enabled him to create some form of musical sound (Ezek. 28:13). Some scholars believe Satan was the primary worship leader in heaven before his fall.

What are cherubim, and what was their original purpose? Ezekiel gives a more detailed description of a cherub than any other prophet. Ezekiel's vision reveals an interesting picture of specific details and features of the cherubim. First, they have the likeness of a man (Ezek. 1:5) which, as we continue reading, seems to refer to facial appearance and general bodily form.

Ezekiel noticed the cherubim were given four wings (Ezek. 1:6). The description of their feet is quite strange (Ezek. 1:7), as they are straight, the color of burnished brass, and like the hoofs of calves—thus explaining the early name given by old timers for Satan: splitfoot.

Under their wings are hands that appeared as the hands of men (Ezek. 1:8). The prophet observed the cherubim's outward color was as "burning coals of fire" (Ezek. 1:13), which is an orange-red glowing color. These cherubim move so swiftly that lightning flashes follow them (Ezek. 1:13, 14). Could this be why Christ said, *"I beheld Satan like lightning fall from heaven*" (Luke 10:18), referring to the swiftness of his fall from the upper celestial realm?

Based on Ezekiel's vision, the cherubim have four faces: an ox, an eagle, a lion and a man (1:10). Compare this insight with John's vision in Revelation 4, of the four heavenly living creatures. These also have four faces: an ox, eagle, lion and man (Rev. 4:7), meaning that these living creatures in Revelation are cherubim. These four angels give glory to God and continually cry, "Holy, Holy, Holy," which was the *original* purpose of a cherub.

These same four cherubim (called "beasts" in the KJV) were directly involved in showing John future apocalyptic events and judgments to unfold upon the earth. There are four different "beasts," and in chapter 6, each of these four beasts says to John, "Come and see." They show John four different scenes with four horses of different colors and their riders (Rev. 6:1-8). Thus, Christ allowed these four heavenly cherubim, who have worshipped God from the beginning of time, to reveal aspects of the future to the Apostle John.

What do the four faces of cherubim—ox, eagle, lion, and man—symbolize? Some note that these four faces can represent the fourfold ministry manifestations of Christ as revealed in the four gospels:

Heavenly Emblem	Imagery of Christ	Gospel Reference
The head of a lion	Jesus the Lion of Judah	Matthew's Gospel
The head of an ox	Jesus the Servant	Mark's Gospel
The head of a man	Jesus the Son of Man	Luke's Gospel
The head of an eagle	Jesus the Eternal Word	John's Gospel

I believe Satan was the *first* created cherub, and the four faces reveal the spiritual corruption he introduced when he was expelled from the heavenly kingdom. At his fall, the four faces that were once positive became four negatives. The face of a *lion* represents Satan as the roaring lion seeking whom he may devour (1 Pet. 5:8). The face of an *eagle* marks him as the "prince of the power of the air" (Eph. 2:2), since the eagle is known as a powerful bird that dominates the air. The *ox* is a strong beast that lives much of its life under a yoke, reminding us that Satan brings people under a yoke of spiritual bondage and sin they are unable to break on their own (Isa. 10:27). The fourth face of a *man* is simply the face of temptation, as men continually deal with temptations that are often introduced to us through the influence of others (2 Tim. 4:17).

The first mention of cherubim was after Adam and Eve were expelled from the garden. At Eden's east entrance, God placed cherubim and a flaming sword that turned in all directions. This was done to prevent man from entering the center of the garden and eating from the tree of life, thus living forever in a sinful condition (Gen 3:24). This event poses several unanswerable questions, including: When did these cherubim stop guarding the tree of life? What happened to the tree of life and tree of the knowledge of good and evil?

Eden's original location is unknown and marked only by tradition; and obviously, the cherubim at the tree have long been decommissioned from their guardianship. Perhaps God removed the tree during the flood of Noah, when the giants perished, fallen angels were confined, and the landscape of the entire earth was transformed. The answer to these questions will remain a mystery for the time being.

OTHER TYPES OF ANGELS

The Scripture reveals numerous names and types of angels. *Cherubim* are assigned as guardians of the Divine Presence. There are *seraphim* (Isa. 6:1-6), or angels whose name implies a "burning" from their copper color. There are *archangels*, meaning a chief angel in authority and position. The only archangel who is named in the Bible is Michael (Jude 9).

Some of the most unique angelic creatures presently surround the throne of God. There are four of them, again with the faces of an ox, an eagle, a lion, and a man. Each individual creature has six wings that are covered with eyes. Their assignment is to proclaim with a loud voice, "Holy, holy, holy is the Lord God Almighty, which was, and is, and is to come" (Rev. 4:8).

Ministering spirits are angels assigned for the personal ministry of believers (Heb. 1:4). These represent various types of angels involved in heavenly and earthly ministry in ages present.

Two categories of angels are lesser known, yet were active in ages past—the *sons of God* and the *morning stars*. In Job we read:

> "Where were you when I laid the foundations of the earth?
> Tell Me, if you have understanding.
> Who determined its measurements?
> Surely you know!
> Or who stretched the line upon it?
> To what were its foundations fastened?
> Or who laid its cornerstone,
> When the morning stars sang together,
> And all the sons of God shouted for joy?
>
> – Job 38:4-7 (NKJV)

The phrase "sons of God" is found in the Old Testament five times (Gen. 6:2, 4; Job 1:6; 2:1; 38:7). The Hebrew phrase is *bene-Elohim*. In Genesis 6:2, a remnant of these "sons of God" had sexual union with the daughters of men, and procreated a strange breed of giant men:

> "Now it came to pass, when men began to multiply on the face of the earth, and daughters were born to them, that the sons of God saw the daughters of men, that they were beautiful; and they took wives for themselves of all whom they chose.
>
> "And the LORD said, "My Spirit shall not strive with man forever, for he is indeed flesh; yet his days shall be one hundred and twenty years."
>
> "There were giants on the earth in those days, and also afterward, when the sons of God came in to the daughters of men and they bore children to them. Those were the mighty men who were of old, men of renown.
>
> – Genesis 6:1-4 (NKJV)

Some scholars say these were simply Adam's descendants (men) who turned wicked and procreated a wicked seed on the earth. However, it is biologically impossible for normal men and women to produce men as tall as Goliath (between ten to thirteen feet tall, depending upon the measurement of a cubit).

The Hebrew word *giants* in Genesis 6:4 is *nephilim*, meaning "he fell." The name implies something or someone who fell; and in the context of Genesis 6:4, it refers to the fallen angels who produced an offspring of wicked, giant men. Biblical and historical records indicate that giants were the offspring of fallen angels. These giants were called "mighty men of renown." According to the early church fathers, the existence of these giants formed the embellishments of the "gods" in Greek mythology.

The Encyclopedia Judaica says this under Angels and Angelology:

> "The earliest report of fallen angels is found in the book of Enoch. The sons of heaven, who belonged to the guardian angels, had lusted for the beauty of the daughters of men and, in the time of Jared, decided to descend upon Mount Hermon to carry out their plans from there. There were two hundred of them, and their leader made them swear an oath to adhere to their purpose and it was this oath that gave the mountain its name—Hermon."

> "They consorted with the daughters of men, who birthed a generation of giants who set about mercilessly destroying human beings. The fallen angels also taught men the use of weapons and other tools promoting immorality and crime. In this manner demonic wisdom came into being, in addition to Divine wisdom, and led to the corruption of mankind."

> – ENCYCLOPEDIA JUDAICA PAGE 966

Justin Martyr commented on fallen angels' involvement in producing giants when he penned:

> "Moved by man's outcry, the four archangels appealed to God and were given orders to punish the fallen angels.

> "(God) committed the care of men and all things under heaven to angels whom he appointed over them. But the angels transgressed this appointment, and were captivated by the love of women, and begot children who were those that are called demons; and besides, they afterwards subdued the human race to themselves, partly by teaching them to offer sacrifices, and

incense and libations, of which they stood in need after they were enslaved by lustful passions; and among them they sowed murders, wars, adulteries, intemperate deeds, and all wickedness.

"Whence also the poets and mythologists, not knowing that it was the angels and those demons whom had been begotten by them, did these things to men, and women, and cities, and nations which they related, ascribed them to god himself, and to the offspring of those who were called brothers, Neptune and Pluto, and to the children again of these their offspring. For whatever name each of the angels had given himself and his children, by that name they were called them."

— JUSTIN MARTYR (BOOK 1 PAGE 190)

In Job 38:4-7, God revealed that when He created the heavens and the earth, both the "sons of God" and the "morning stars" rejoiced during creation as they observed God laying the earth's foundation. The phrase *sons of God* in this context refers to angels (also mentioned in Genesis 6:4), and are connected to the pre-flood generation, which was 1,658 years from Adam. The *morning stars*, a second team of angels, are also referred to in ages past, at the time of creation (Job 38:7). Both groups were angels, and both groups had a specific number within their own ranks that fell into Satan's rebellious scheme, which was exposed by the Almighty sometime after the initial creation of heaven and earth (Gen. 1:1).

I believe that in ages past, Satan was the angel overseeing and given authority over the *morning stars*, thus having his own group of angels under his command. Michael was the chief archangel over the *sons of God*, as he too has his own angels under his authority. This is clear when John spoke of "Satan and his angels and Michael and his angels" (see Rev. 12:7-9).

The writer of Job peered into the spirit realm and observed a heavenly council meeting with God, Satan and the "sons of God," who were standing before God in His heavenly throne center. The sons of God were angelic messengers, and they may be the same heavenly host observed by the prophet Micaiah, who saw the "host of heaven" standing on the left and right side of God's throne, making a decision to set up Ahab to fall in a battle that resulted in his death (2 Chron. 18:18-22).

According to sacred Jewish history, the Almighty sent a group of angels—identified as the sons of God—from heaven to earth, where they took on the form of human men to live among the people and teach them righteousness. For some, the idea of a spirit being becoming flesh is impossible. However, we read in Scripture that angels have appeared in human form at times, and Hebrews 13:2 tells us that angels can appear as strangers, and we will not be aware they are angels. Consider the two angels who visited Sodom (Gen. 19). Consider Jacob, who wrestled a man all night, only to later discover the man was an angel (Gen. 32:24-30). The miracle of the incarnation of Christ illustrates how a spirit being in heaven (Christ pre-existed with God), can become flesh and be called the "Son of God" (John 1:14; Luke 1:35).

Jewish writings teach that these angels, over time, became enamored with the daughters of men and impregnated the women, who gave birth to genetic offspring that were larger than normal humans called giants. Clement of Alexander gives a narrative on the pre-flood angels that came to earth and produced the offspring of giants:

> "For the spirits who inhabit the heaven, the angels who dwell in the lowest region, being grieved at the ingratitude of men to God, asked that they might enter into the life of men, that, really by becoming men, by more intercourse they might convict those who had acted ungratefully toward him.

> "But when, having assumed these forms, they convicted as covetous those who stole them, and changed themselves into the nature of men, in order that, living holily, and showing the possibility of so living, they might subject the ungrateful to punishment, yet having become in all respects men, they also partook of human lust, and being brought under its subjection they fell into cohabitation with women; and being involved with them...for the fire itself extinguished by the weight of lust and changed into the flesh, they trod the impious path downward."

> – ANTE-NICENE FATHERS; CLEMENT OF ALEXANDER;
> BOOK VIII, CHAPTER VI, PAGE 272

Clement added commentary in a section called, "Their Discoveries," that these fallen angels also taught men the use of metals, charms, precious stones, magic and astrology, and were called "demons bound in the flesh."

In a Jewish writing called the book of Jubilees (fragments were discovered in Qumran), the writer states that God, in His anger, uprooted the fallen angels and instructed they be imprisoned in the depths of the earth, where they remain in this secluded prison, separated from mankind. These are the angels referred to in Jude 6 and in 2 Peter 2:4 that did not keep their original state, but sinned.

TABLETS REVEAL THE 'GODS CAME DOWN'

While the idea of angels coming down and corrupting mankind seems odd, ancient secular records also speak of such unusual events. The area of ancient Mesopotamia—today the region of Syria and Iraq—is the site of the earliest known civilizations, including the Sumerians, who dwelt in this fertile region along the Euphrates River over 5,000 years ago. Archeologists have discovered numerous clay cuneiform tablets and cylinder seals from early inhabitants that describe stories of the "gods" who descended to earth, lived among men, and created a massive race of demi-gods.

One tale, called the Epic of Creation, is etched on seven tablets and begins with a group of gods who arrived from a planet millions of years old, and were assigned to live on earth among men. The gods (which in the Biblical narrative would have been angels) took earthly females as wives and produced a race of demi-gods (part human and part god). The text mentions a group called the Anunnaki (a name which some suggest is linked to the Biblical race of giants called Anakim in Deut. 2:11), which originated and lived in the region of the former Garden of Eden.

According to cuneiform tablets from Ur and Sumeria, one of the demi-god sons was named Marduk, who was believed to be of the race of giants born through the fallen angels living in Sumaria. Interestingly, in the time of king Nebuchadnezzar, who reconstructed and expanded Babylon to empire status, one of the chief idols was named Marduk.

In my antiquities collection is a baked clay tablet the size of a man's hand, which is over four thousand years old and originated from the region of Mesopotamia. On the tablet is the imagery of a very tall man dressed in attire similar to the ancient kings of Chaldea and Mesopotamia. He is standing behind a platform of some type, with what appears to be several men bowing before the king-type figure. The oddity is that the "king" is three times larger than the others on the tablet. While it cannot be proven, it is possible this is an historical record of one of the giants that existed and was worshipped in the early days—since giants also pro-created for a limited time after Noah's flood until the time of King David (2 Sam. 21:16-22). This object was found near Ur, in the same territory where Abraham once lived.

Ur of Chaldea was the land just south of the former tower of Babel, where a tall ziggurat was built by Nimrod in the early city of Babel (Gen. 11). Ur was the city from which God told Abraham to depart (Gen. 11:28-31). Cuneiform tablets unearthed from the ruins of ancient Ur are some of the oldest known writings of mankind. Numerous tablets speak of gods who rode to earth coming from the stars. Ancient Akkadian tablets include stories of the gods who are connected with the stars.

Remember that in Eden, God Himself literally descended to earth for an unknown time, where He met with Adam at the tree of life (Gen. 3:8). After being expelled from the center of the garden, the entrance to the Tree of Life was also guarded by a cherub, which was visibly seen by Adam and Eve (Gen. 3:24) and perhaps their descendants. Eden's narrative indicates that both *God and angels* had direct access to earth during mankind's early beginnings.

AREN'T ANGELS GENDERLESS?

In the past, when teaching on this subject of angels taking on the form of flesh, becoming men, and procreating a satanic seed on earth called giants, the first challenge is the comment, "Angels are sexless and therefore unable to perform sexual acts, so this is all a myth." This idea is usually based on Matthew 22:28-30, where the question was asked, that if a woman was married seven times and all her husbands died, then whose wife would she be in the resurrection? Christ replied, "For in the resurrection they neither marry, nor are given in marriage, but are as the angels of God in heaven."

Male angels are always addressed with the pronoun he, meaning they are masculine (for example, Michael and his angels, Rev. 12:7). If all angels are masculine beings, then they will not be married in heaven.

One Scripture penned by the prophet Zechariah has initiated a brisk theological debate. The prophet saw a vision of two angels flying with a basket. He wrote:

> "Then lifted I up mine eyes, and looked, and behold there came out two women, and the wind was in their wings; for they had wings like the wings of a stork: and they lifted up the ephah between the earth and the heaven."
>
> - ZECHARIAH 5:9

These two "women," with wings similar to storks, were carrying a basket that concealed a wicked woman inside, and they sat it on a foundation in the land of Shinar. While one verse may not be sufficient to prove this possibility, it is interesting that these angelic creatures had the appearance of two *women* and not the normal appearance of *men*, such as the two angels at Christ's tomb that were identified as men, and the two "men in white" who predicted Christ's return (Luke 24:4; Acts 1:10).

Christ pre-existed in the beginning with God, eventually came to earth in flesh, and was tempted with the same temptations as you and I; yet He never sinned (Heb. 4:15). While being clothed in flesh, the Adamic sin nature is in the human bloodline, thus giving all people the *potential* to sin. However, Christ exercised the power over the potential to sin by submitting to the influence and control of the Holy Spirit.

The mystery of angelic and human beings pro-creating giants that were considered gods among men might not be fully understood in contemporary theology. Yet, both Biblical and other religious history reveals that the sons of God were the angels sent from heaven to earth to teach men righteousness. They failed in their assignment and, instead, procreated a "seed of the serpent"—a population of giants that corrupted the imaginations of mankind (Gen. 6:5) and moved God to wipe out most of humanity with a universal flood (Gen. 7 and 8).

I believe the *morning star angels* were aligned with Satan when he was positioned as the premier, first creation angel who was given the exalted title of *the anointed cherub*. He was covered with brightness (Ezek. 28:17) and, as you will see later in the book, literally sparkled with stones that formed his covering—or in Hebrew, his "garnishing" (Ezek. 28:13). In the ancient past, a group of these angels were cast from heaven, along with Satan. The entire cosmos reflected the spiritual darkness that engulfed the universe, as after Satan's expulsion, darkness is seen covering the surface (face) of the earth (Gen. 1:2).

God stepped into the cosmos and created the heavens and earth (Gen. 1:1), but after Satan's rebellion and the collapse of unity among the heavenly host, darkness covered the face of the earth. Over time, God's supernatural light pierced the darkness and initiated a new creation on the earth, including the formation of a man named Adam, also called the "son of God" (Luke 3:38).

In Genesis 1:3, the great light covering the earth was not the sun, moon or stars, as they were created on the fourth day of the creation narrative (Gen. 1:16-19). This mysterious early light has been called by rabbis the primal light of creation—an unknown brilliance from the upper world that shattered the black space that covered the future, lower earth world.

In the gospel of John, beginning with chapter 1:1-14, the apostle describes early creation from a view noted by Hebrew mystics. The first five verses begin:

> "In the beginning was the Word, and the Word was with God, and the Word was God. He was in the beginning with God. All things were made through Him, and without Him nothing was made that was made. In Him was life, and the life was the light

of men. And the light shined in the darkness, and the darkness did not comprehend it."

– JOHN 1:1-5 (NKJV)

The "beginning" alludes to ages past; before, during and after creation as recorded in Genesis 1:1. The light shining in darkness points back to creation, when the earth was covered in darkness (Gen. 1:2) and a mysterious light exploded onto the planet. John said the world was made by Him (John 1:10), and He was the light of the world (John 1:9). It was Christ who was the first light of creation and came to earth to break the darkness of sin over mankind. The Almighty clearly *replaced the fallen star morning star with a new morning star*, as Christ now bears the title, Morning Star:

> "I, Jesus, have sent My angel to testify to you these things in the churches. I am the Root and the Offspring of David, the Bright and Morning Star."

– REVELATION 22:16

> "And I will give him the morning star."

– REVELATION 2:28

In astronomical terms, the *morning star* pertains to the first star seen in the morning (often identified with the planet Venus). At the time of the second temple, the early sun rising over the Mount of Olives signaled a new day at the sacred temple. Christ, the new Morning Star, now has a family both in heaven and on earth (Eph. 3:15). Our position in Christ's kingdom is "sons of God!" We have replaced the fallen angels and now are considered sons! We read:

> "Beloved, now are we the sons of God, and it doth not yet appear what we shall be: but we know that, when he shall appear, we shall be like him; for we shall see him as he is."

– 1 JOHN 3:2

In Scripture, there is a time identified as the "fullness of the Gentiles" (Rom. 11:25). Paul wrote that a large majority of the natural seed of Abraham would remain in spiritual blindness toward Christ being their Messiah, until the fullness of the Gentiles. Some of the early scholars interpreted this verse to mean that a set number of Gentiles among the nations would hear and receive the Gospel; and once this occurred, God will supernaturally remove the scales from Israel's eyes and many will receive Christ as Messiah.

Some have suggested the number of Gentile converts would replace the number of fallen angels; and when this number is complete, the end of the age will come. There is no Biblical proof for this interpretation. However, we are told by Paul that the whole creation is groaning in anticipation for the manifestation of the sons of God (Rom. 8:19). This "sons of God" refers, not to angelic beings, but to men and women who have believed upon Christ and will manifest His kingdom on the earth.

WHAT DOES SATAN LOOK LIKE?

Jesus informed His disciples that He and the Father are one, and whoever saw Him was also seeing the Father (John 10:30; 14:9). When Christ forgave the woman caught in adultery, Christ was revealing the love of God toward sinners (John 8:1-11). When He reached out to touch a leper (which was forbidden in the Law), He was expressing God's love toward the untouchable (Mark 1:40-44).

When Christ took five loaves and two fish to multiply a lad's lunch and feed thousands, He was demonstrating God's concern for the hungry and those who needed provision to sustain themselves (Luke 9:13-17).

When Christ cast out evil spirits from those who desired deliverance from their control, He was once again acting out what His Father had performed in ages past; that is, removing Satan and his cohorts from places they did not belong and were not welcomed. The motivation for Christ's ministry was love, for God Himself is love (1 John 4:8).

Years ago, when I was speaking to a group of precious ladies who were part of a drug and alcohol recovery program, I had a very moving experience. I asked God why the adversary was intent on capturing men and women, and placing them into the bondage of an addictive lifestyle through drugs and alcohol. I heard the Holy Spirit say, "Satan knows that men and women are created in God's image. His desire is to mar the image of God that he sees in each person. Chemical substances and alcohol alter the personality and emotions, and they change the image of God and prevent the person from being an overcomer who is in covenant with God."

When I see one of God's creations, male or female, young or old, bearing the weight of an addiction that is wrecking their mind, body and spirit, I see Satan at work. When a father physically abuses his wife and children, bruising their bodies and wounding their souls, Satan is at work. As a young man is handcuffed and led into prison for a heinous crime, knowing that his life is ruined and his future is a concrete room behind iron bars, I see the success of Satan.

If you want to know what Satan looks like, just look around at the hate, racism, fear, bondage and addiction, and look into the faces of the victims. You will see two faces—the image of God and a face under the dominion of the adversary.

Satan the Transformer

Perhaps we will never know, until the great white throne judgment, what Satan actually looks like. Nor does it really matter. It is his *actions* and *evil activity* that must be exposed and dealt with. One of the most important warfare keys for any believer to seize and understand is that Satan is a master transformer. We read:

> "For such are false apostles, deceitful workers, transforming themselves into apostles of Christ. And no wonder! For Satan himself transforms himself into an angel of light. Therefore it is no great thing if his ministers also transform themselves into ministers of righteousness, whose end will be according to their works."
>
> – 2 Corinthians 11:13-15 (NJKV)

In Greek, the word for transformed (KJV) means to *transfigure* or to *disguise*. For example, various insects and reptiles can camouflage their skins and look exactly like their surroundings (grass, weeds, wood, or rocks). They are often undetected with the naked eye until a person observes their movement.

Satan comes to steal, kill, and destroy (John 10:10). Yet, if he appeared as a thief, murderer or destroyer, most people on the planet would want no contact with him whatsoever. They would guard their homes, protect their families, and avoid him in every way possible. Therefore, he will never appear in any form that might expose him for what he is.

Instead of appearing as a killer, he comes bearing "gifts" that lead to addictions and death. Instead of showing himself as a thief, he slides in as your best friend, one who truly "understands you," but who wears a disguise to hide his real intention, which is to rob you of eternal life. Those who are blinded by sin cannot see their final destruction, because the adversary masks his identity and true intentions.

Having ministered face-to-face to sinners of all types in congregations around the world, I can think of many words to expose Satan's nature, thinking patterns, and strategies. One word that always comes to mind is *separation*. Satan is a separator. The first sin to enter the universe originated with him and caused a split among the kingdom of the angels. He then separated Adam and Eve from God after they were tempted and sinned. Later, he separated two brothers, Cain and Abel, and planted jealousy to motivate Cain to slay his brother. And this activity occurred in just the first four chapters of Genesis!

Sin acts as a separator, and Satan gave birth to sin when iniquity was found in him. The adversary will do anything possible to separate you from your friends and family, and most of all, to separate you from God.

CHAPTER 5

Stones of Fire

MANY CHRISTIANS ASSUME that, since God had no beginning, both the cosmic heavens and the heavenly city New Jerusalem have always existed. In Genesis, Moses informed the reader that, "In the beginning God created the heaven..." (Gen. 1:1). John wrote that the holy city was "prepared as a bride adorned for her husband" (Rev. 21:2). God prepared heaven, earth, mankind, the animal kingdom, and all things were made by Him (John 1:3).

The Scripture says that God prepared the future, including the kingdom itself, from the foundation of the world (Matt. 25:34). The *foundation* of the world refers to the countless ages past, when God was creating the heaven and the earth, and can also allude to the earliest stages of the first man, Adam, when he occupied the Garden of Eden before his fall.

Christ revealed mysteries (parables) that had been concealed in God from the foundation of the world (Matt. 13:35). During His deep intercession in Gethsemane's garden just prior to His arrest, Christ confessed that the heavenly Father had loved Him "before the foundation of the world" (John 17:24). The Book of Life, a heavenly register holding the names of the righteous, existed from the foundation of the world (Rev. 13:8).

The idea of events "from the foundation of the world" is also important in prophetic judgments, as when Christ warned that His generation was coming under a curse for shedding the blood of righteous men and prophets. Christ said, "That the blood of all the prophets, which was shed from the foundation of the world, may be required of this generation" (Luke 11:50). This indicates there were prophets, "from the foundation (beginning) of the world."

The next verse speaks of the blood of Abel (v-51), who was the first righteous man to be slain by his brother Cain. This murder occurred at the very early stages of Adam's life, which was the *foundation or the beginning* of the world that we now live in. Enoch was a prophet and the seventh man from Adam, and he provided an early example of prophetic utterances during the first one thousand years of man's dominion on earth.

The kingdom of heaven was prepared (Matt. 25:34) from the foundation of the world. Thus in ages past, during the earliest stages of creating the heavens and the earth, and before the creation of man, God was preparing a *city* and a *kingdom* in heaven. Some may assume that God simply spoke the Holy City, the New Jerusalem, into existence. The New Jerusalem was not spoken into being, however, but was *built and made* under God's supervision.

Note also that God did not *speak* man into existence and say, let there be a man, and there was a man; but God said, *"Let us make man"* (Gen. 1:26). God *formed man* and *breathed into his nostrils*, and man became a living soul (Gen. 2:7). God *made* and *formed* the first human on the planet, instead of just *speaking him* into existence, as was His pattern in the earthly creation narrative. Likewise, God prepared and made a place in heaven—a city for the citizens of His kingdom!

The New Jerusalem was also prepared (made) by the Lord *before the foundation of world*. We know it existed in Abraham's time, for we read, *"For he looked for the city which has foundations, whose builder and maker is God"* (Heb. 11:10). God speaks, God makes, and God builds. The New Jerusalem was created in ages past, but completed long before the time of Abraham.

Some will contradict this statement, saying that Christ stated He was going back to heaven to prepare a place for us, and that, in this place He was going to build mansions:

> "Let not your heart be troubled: ye believe in God, believe also in me. In my Father's house are many mansions: if it were not so,

I would have told you. I go to prepare a place for you. And if I go and prepare a place for you, I will come again, and receive you unto myself; that where I am, there ye may be also."

– JOHN 14:1-3

Read the verse carefully. First, Christ revealed that, "in my Father's house are many mansions" (or dwelling places), meaning they were *already in existence* at the time Christ was speaking. When Christ said He was preparing a place for us, He was referring to more than the preparation of heavenly dwelling places. He prepared a place for us to be with God eternally, and gave us access directly to the Father through His blood. *"I will come again to receive you to myself"* (v-3) refers to the gathering together and the resurrection of the dead in Christ—an event revealed in 1 Thessalonians 4:16-17.

In the context of the redemptive covenant on the cross, before the resurrection of Christ, all righteous souls at death were taken to a chamber under the earth called Abraham's bosom (Luke 16:22). However, after the resurrection and redemptive work of Christ, we received a double blessing. First, we now have access to God directly, without the need for an earthly high priest, as Christ now serves in the heavenly temple as our High Priest. Second, when we die, our soul and spirit is now transported upward, into the paradise section of heaven, where we will rest until the resurrection of the dead in Christ, when Christ returns.

The words of John 14:1-3 were spoken by Christ on earth nearly two thousand years ago, meaning that at that time, the dwelling places in the New Jerusalem were already prepared. In fact, the heavenly city and God's temple are all a part of the kingdom of God. The kingdom was "prepared from the foundation of the world," or from the early creation (Matt. 25:34). Paul wrote concerning God creating all things and said, "...the works were finished from the foundation of the world" (Heb. 4:3).

God knew that angels would rebel. He knew that man would also rebel; thus God planned the crucifixion of Christ "from the foundation of the world" (Rev. 13:8). The Almighty even prepared a city registry for names of the righteous, "from the foundation of the world"

(Rev. 17:8). Every detail providing for the future was prepared from the very beginning.

HEAVEN: BEFORE THE FOUNDATION OF THE WORLD

Before the beginning of the cosmic and earthy creation recorded by Moses in Genesis 1:2 through 2:25, the third heaven, the eternal abode of the Almighty, already existed. In fact, angels were present at the time God laid the foundation of the earth. Job identified them as "sons of God" and "morning stars":

> "Where were you when I laid the foundations of the earth? Tell Me, if you have understanding. Who determined its measurements? Surely you know! Or who stretched the line upon it? To what were its foundations fastened? Or who laid its cornerstone, when the morning stars sang together, and all the sons of God shouted for joy?"
>
> – JOB 38:4-7

The phrase, *sons of God* in Hebrew is *ben Elohim*, and I have already mentioned that, in several Old Testament passages, it refers to a specific type of angelic being (Gen. 6:2, 4; Job 1:6; 2:1; 38:7). The second term, *morning stars*, is interesting because the word *morning* in Hebrew is *boqer* and it means the *breaking of dawn*. The word *stars*, to the western mind, immediately brings thoughts of the cosmic heavens and the millions of shimmering dots of light that can be seen in the sky at night. In the Old Testament, the word *stars* is used in thirty-five Scriptures, and is primarily translated to mean stars in the celestial sphere, including the constellations (Isa. 13:10; Amos 5:8; Ps. 147:4).

However, there are a few instances in which the word *stars* is used *figuratively* as an *angelic being*, or a *strong angel*. In Revelation 9:1, a "star falls from heaven with a key to the abyss." This is not an asteroid falling from the sky, but an angel descending to earth. The same is true with the Old Testament word *host*, which can have three meanings: a large army of men (Exod. 14:17); the sun, moon, and stars of heaven (Isa. 34:4); or an innumerable company of angels (1 Kings 22:19, Dan. 8:10-11).

When God concluded His creation, we read, "Thus the heavens and the earth were finished, and all the host of them" (Gen. 2:1). This Hebrew word *host* is *tsaba'* and by definition means "a mass of persons." Figuratively this can mean "a massive group organized for war." Since the only mass number of people or things that existed from the foundation of the world were the angels that were present at creation, then this passage could be identifying specific angels as warring angels. God knew that Adam's fall would initiate a cosmic battle for humanity, so God prepared His army before the battle began.

The concept of warring angels is Biblical. The premier warring angel is identified as Michael the archangel (Jude 9). The word *archangel* means *a chief angel,* one which possesses authority far above others. After Moses's death, Michael intervened, and wrestled Satan over the body of Moses, possibly to prevent Satan from seizing the corpse, but also to prevent the people from discovering where Moses' body was buried (Jude 9). Michael is marked as the chief guardian prince over the nation of Israel (Dan. 12:1).

In the future and final battle of the ages, a cosmic conflict will shake the heavens once again. Then Michael and *his angels* will engage Satan and *his angels* in a heavenly clash that concludes with Satan's expulsion from the second heaven to the earth (Rev. 12:7-10).

THE SECRETS OF THE MORNING STARS

Since the Hebrew word *morning* refers to the *breaking of day* and the word *stars* figuratively refers to *angels,* the phrase could allude to angels of the morning. When Isaiah penned his prophecy about the destruction of the King of Babylon (see chapter 14), scholars note that several statements appear to conceal a double application or a dual prophecy. The first referred to the natural, earthly king of Babylon. The second referred to a supernatural prince spirit—none other than Satan himself—that controlled the king of Babylon, and still holds a grip on the kingdoms of this world (see Luke 4:6).

In Isaiah 14:12, the English Bible translators used the word *Lucifer,* identifying him as the "son of the morning." In Hebrew, this word *Lucifer* is the Hebrew word *heylel,* and is translated *morning star.* It reads,

"How are you fallen from heaven, O Lucifer, son of the morning." The Hebrew root word of heylel means to *have light or brightness.*

There is a certain light that this fallen angel Lucifer, or Satan, still carries. The Apostle Paul, in his letter to the church at Corinth, warned believers that false apostles and deceitful workers could transform themselves into apostles of Christ, or appear to be something they are not. Paul warned, *"For Satan himself transforms himself into an angel of light"* (2 Cor. 11:14). Satan's ability to use light, including what we would term "spiritual illumination," to deceive humanity is seen throughout the world today. Two world religions, Islam and Mormonism, are both based upon revelations allegedly given to their founders by an angelic messenger.

In Islam, the angelic visitor (whom Muhammad believed to be Gabriel), allegedly told Mohammad that Allah has no son. However, in the Bible, the angel Gabriel told Mary that Jesus would be "called the Son of God" (Luke 1:35). Herein we see a major contradiction, and the primary argument that Muslims use against Christianity.

The angel who allegedly gave Joseph Smith gold plates to translate also introduced revelation that is contrary to Scripture. This is why the traditional Christian faith has criticized the book of Mormon and exposed its fallacies.

The reason for bringing up these two religious examples is that Paul warned:

> "But even if we, or an angel from heaven, preach any other gospel to you than what we have preached to you, let him be accursed. As we have said before, so now I say again, if anyone preaches any other gospel to you than what you have received, let him be accursed."
>
> – GAL. 1:8-9 (NKJV)

In all world religions, especially Buddhism, the followers speak of illumination and commonly mention light. Light can be either natural or supernatural. Each morning when the sun peeks over the horizon we call it the breaking of dawn. The morning star theme is important as, in the book of Revelation, Christ is presently the bright and morning star (Rev. 2:28; 22:16), indicating that He is the true light that illuminates all men. This makes Him the light of the world (John 9:5).

Christ pre-existed with God at the very beginning of creation, as we read that "in the beginning was the Word," (John 1:1) and, "all things were made by Him" (John 1:3). Before Christ was called the bright and morning star, the one angel—perhaps the first one ever created, known today as Satan—was formed to be the *great light bearer* in the heavenly temple.

The prophet Ezekiel calls this created being "the anointed cherub that covers." He was "on the holy mountain of God" (Ezek. 28:14). Ezekiel understood that this cherub was also in "Eden the garden of God" (Ezek. 28:13). Paul revealed there is a heavenly paradise (garden) located in the third heaven (2 Cor. 12:4), and Moses recorded the name of man's pre-sin garden as the "Garden in Eden."

A serpent beguiled Eve into acting against God's instruction, thus bringing sin into the earth (Gen. 3:1-6). After Adam and Eve were expelled from Eden, God assigned a guardian cherub with a flaming sword to protect the entrance to the gates of Eden and prevent the couple from returning to the tree of life where they might eat of the tree and live forever in a sinful condition (Gen. 3:22).

Twice in Ezekiel, we are informed of the magnificent beauty of this angelic creature called the *anointed cherub*. We read where he was "perfect in beauty" (Ezek. 28:12) and "perfect in all his ways" (28:15). Again we are told, "Because of your beauty, you have corrupted your wisdom by reason of your brightness" (28:17). What made him so beautiful? After all, there are numerous types of angels, and many are unusual and quite fearful in their appearance.

Ezekiel detailed how the anointed cherub was "perfect in all his ways until iniquity was found in him" (28:15), and He was "cast out of the holy mountain" (28:16). Christ described Satan's quick removal from heaven as lightning, indicating the swiftness of his removal from God's presence (Luke 10:18). The reason for his expulsion from heaven was that his heart was lifted up in pride (28:17). Ezekiel's insight also confirms Isaiah's revelation of ages past, when he pierced the veil of eternity and saw what was in the heart of Lucifer:

> "How you are fallen from heaven, O Lucifer, son of the morning! How you are cut down to the ground, you who weakened the nations! For you have said in your heart: 'I will ascend into heaven, I will exalt my throne above the stars of God; I will also sit on the mount of the congregation on the farthest sides of the north; I will ascend above the heights of the clouds, I will be like the Most High.' Yet you shall be brought down to Sheol, to the lowest depths of the pit."
>
> – ISAIAH 14:12-15

Both Isaiah and Ezekiel provide the best commentary on the fall of this anointed cherub from heaven. In the context, Ezekiel rebuked the wealthy, arrogant prince of Tyre, whose name was Ithbaal. Ezekiel provided a summary of the king's wealth (Ezekiel 27) and exposed the danger of his pride and earthly wisdom that made him popular and wealthy (Ezek. 28:1-5).

In the midst of the warning to this king, Ezekiel peered into the past and compared the future fall of king Ithbaal, who believed he was a god (Ezek. 28:2), with the demise of another high-ranking being that once served as a ruling angel, thought he was a god, and desired to sit on the mountain of God and literally seize God's throne for himself (Isa. 14:12-14).

However, this cherub was violently excommunicated from the family of angels and hurled off the holy mountain in heaven (Luke 10:18), just as *this king* would also be brought down to the pit (Isa. 14:15; Ezek. 28:8).

In Isaiah, the *pit* which Lucifer will be cast into is the Hebrew word *bowr*, meaning a pit, a hole as a cistern, or a prison. Centuries later, John saw Satan being cast into the bottomless pit in Revelation 20:3. The earthly king of Tyre is cast into the pit, the Hebrew word being *shachath*, meaning a *pit of destruction*. For Satan, it will be the bottomless pit where he will be confined for a thousand years (Rev. 20:1-2).

In Ezekiel, we read that this cherub walked on "stones of fire on the Holy Mountain." This phrase has no reference to the earthly mountain of God in Jerusalem, known as Mount Zion and Mount Moriah, called the "holy mountain," (Isa. 11:9; 56:7; 65:25), as in Ezekiel's day, the Babylonians had destroyed Jerusalem and the Temple, or the holy mountain. Also, the walls and the sacred buildings were cut from limestone in Solomon's time. No fire was used in the building process, and no precious stones were on the walls, although precious stones were given to Solomon as a gift and placed in the Temple treasury (1 Kings 10:2; 1 Chron. 29:8).

Early church fathers commented on this passage and believed Ezekiel was speaking, not of a human king, but of the cherub who led a rebellion:

> "This description, it is manifest, properly belongs to the transgression of the angel, and not to the prince; for none among human beings was born in the Paradise of God, not even Adam himself, who was rather translated thither nor placed with a cherub on God's holy mountain, that is to say, 'the Heights of Heaven' from which the Lord testifies that Satan fell. It is none else than the very author of sin."
>
> (TURTULLIAN; *THE ANTE-NICENE FATHERS*, VOL. III, PG. 306)

> "This paragraph cannot at all be understood of a man, but of some superior power which had fallen away from the higher position and which had been reduced to a lower and worse condition...We are of the opinion, therefore, that these words were spoken of a certain angel..."
>
> (ORIGEN; *THE ANTE-NICENE FATHERS*; VOL. IV; PG. 259).

The sum of all Biblical evidence that exposes the removal of Satan from heaven, along with a third of the angels that followed him (Rev. 12:4), makes the narrative of Ezekiel's anointed cherub apply to Satan himself. He was, in the beginning, the first created angel; he was given the ability to direct worship; and I believe he was the overseer guardian of the early creation of the heavenly Jerusalem. The stones of fire on the mountain of God allude to the mountain of God in heaven. It is on this mountain that the heavenly Temple rests, and it is where the eternal throne of God and the sacred furniture are also located.

THE STONES IN HEAVEN

In the beginning (ageless past), God created the heavens and the earth (Gen. 1:1). From a void and dark planet covered with water, the Almighty brought forth the mysterious *light* of creation (Gen. 1:3), days prior to the actual formation of the sun, moon and stars (compare Gen. 1:3, the first day, with Gen 1:14-19, the fourth day of creation). From the second through the fifth day, vital life-giving methods to sustain both man and beasts were created by the power of God's spoken word (Gen. chapter 1; Rom. 1:20).

This earthly creation was a reflection of heavenly realities. Throughout the Old Testament, God inspired men to create on earth what already existed in heaven. For example, the sacred gold-covered furniture, such as the Golden Altar, the Ark of the Covenant, and the Golden Candelabra that Moses instructed Bazaleel and Aholiab (Exod. 31: 1-11) to hammer out and forge into seven branches, were all fitted and designed according to a specific pattern God revealed to Moses (Heb. 8:5).

One of the sacred objects created for one man alone, the High Priest, was a special gemstone-studded golden breastplate. It was four-square and held twelve semi-precious and precious gemstones, with each stone representing one of the twelve tribes of Israel, and a tribal name cut into each stone.

The only other covering made with gemstones in the Bible was the covering on the anointed cherub. Ezekiel said that "every precious stone was his covering" (Ezek. 28:13). The Hebrew word *covering* is *mecukkah*, from a root word *cakak,* meaning to entwine as a screen; by implication meaning to fence in and protect.

There are two ways to interpret this covering of nine gemstones. The first is that they could have formed a breastplate covering on the front of his body, just as the twelve gemstones in the gold breastplate covered the heart of the High Priest on his priestly robe of beauty (Ezek. 28). The second interpretation is more unique.

He was the cherub that "covereth." This is interesting, as the word covereth here in Hebrew is *cukkowth*. The English translation is Sukkot, the Hebrew name meaning "booth," or the Hebrew word used for the seventh feast of Israel—the Feast of Tabernacles. The implication is that this angel was involved with some form of tabernacle or important structure in heaven.

When Ezekiel described this angelic creature, he indicated that this special being possessed a gemstone covering, in the form of a breastplate that covered his heart or perhaps his entire body. However, when Ezekiel provided a detailed list of the gemstones on his covering, there were only *nine* stones, instead of *twelve,* as seen on the High Priest's breastplate. Compare the list for the Priest's breastplate in Exodus with the cherub's breastplate in Ezekiel. The High Priest's breastplate contained twelve stones:

> "And thou shalt set in it settings of stones, even four rows of stones: the first row shall be a sardius, a topaz, and a carbuncle: this shall be the first row. And the second row shall be an emerald, a sapphire, and a diamond. And the third row a ligure, an agate, and an amethyst. And the fourth row a beryl, and an onyx, and a jasper: they shall be set in gold in their inclosings."
>
> – Exodus 28:17-20

Here is the anointed cherub's gemstone covering:

> "Thou hast been in Eden the garden of God; every precious stone was thy covering, the sardius, topaz, and the diamond, the beryl, the onyx, and the jasper, the sapphire, the emerald, and the carbuncle, and gold: the workmanship of thy tabrets and of thy pipes was prepared in thee in the day that thou wast created."
>
> – Ezekiel 28:13

Notice the stones that are the same:

High Priest's Breastplate	Covering of the Cherub
sardius	sardius
topaz	topaz
carbuncle	carbuncle
emerald	emerald
sapphire	sapphire
diamond	diamond

ligure (jacinth)	
agate	
amethyst	
beryl	beryl
onyx	onyx
jasper	jasper

When God instructed Moses to build the tabernacle, which would be a dwelling for God to visit His people through the priesthood, the stones placed on the breastplate of the priest are given in a specific order, based upon the birth order of the sons of Jacob. Genesis chapters 29, 30, and 35 reveal the names of the twelve sons of Jacob and the order of their births. Each stone represents one of the twelve tribes of Israel, and here are the names, birth orders, and corresponding gemstones:

Son's Name	Birth Order	Breastplate Gemstone
Reuben	First son (Gen. 29:32)	Sardius
Simeon	Second son (Gen. 29:33)	Topaz
Levi	Third son (Gen. 29:34)	Carbuncle
Judah	Fourth son (Gen. 29:35)	Emerald
Dan	Fifth son (Gen. 30:6)	Sapphire
Naphtali	Sixth son (Gen. 30:8)	Diamond
Gad	Seventh son (Gen. 30:11)	Ligure (jacinth)
Asher	Eighth son (Gen. 30:13)	Agate
Issachar	Ninth son (Gen. 30:18)	Amethyst
Zebulun	Tenth son (Gen. 30:20)	Beryl
Joseph	Eleventh son (Gen. 30:24)	Onyx
Benjamin	Twelfth son (Gen. 35:18)	Jasper

The sardius and the jasper are the *first* and *last* stones on the twelve gemstone breastplate of the High Priest. These two stones represent *Reuben*, the first son of Jacob, and *Benjamin*, his last son. The Hebrew name Reuben means, "behold a son," and the Hebrew name Benjamin means, "son of my right hand." The meanings of Jacob's first and last sons represent Christ, who is also called the first and last (Rev. 1:17). As Reuben, he was introduced on earth as the "Son of God" (Mark 1:1). Today, as the heavenly High Priest, our Benjamin, he is now seated at God's "right hand" (1 Pet. 3:22).

A rainbow is normally a prism of colors, from yellow, to orange, to red, green and blue. In John's vision, the rainbow surrounding the throne is like an *emerald*. On the High Priest's breastplate, the emerald is the fourth stone listed, and Judah was the fourth son born to Jacob; thus the emerald represents the tribe of *Judah*.

The earthly rainbow is a heavenly symbol of a covenant promise God made to Noah, not to again destroy the earth by water (Gen. 9:13-17). Because this bow surrounds the throne and is an emerald (green), this would indicate God's covenant being established with the tribe of Judah—the "emerald" tribe. The Almighty established an everlasting covenant with David, born and raised in the tribe of Judah. He promised that his descendants would sit upon the throne in Jerusalem, and that David himself would, in the future Temple in Jerusalem as the Messiah's assistant, sit as the head of Israel and oversee the twelve tribes from the Holy City, when Messiah returns (Ps. 132:11; Ezek. 37:24-25).

Christ is also called the "Lion of the tribe of Judah" (Rev. 5:5), being born in Bethlehem, the city of David, which was an important tribal city of Judah in Israel's early history. The emerald was also recognized in the Roman period as being a highly valued stone, often used as a wedding gift. However, the fact that the rainbow appears as an emerald carried the connotation (in John's day) of a wedding covenant between the groom—Christ and His bride, the Church!

In the New Testament, the twelve apostles were never given a particular gemstone to represent them, but the names of the twelve apostles are carved on the twelve different gemstone foundations of the city (Rev. 21:14).

The New Testament also provides twelve major doctrines that are the foundation of the faith:

1. Salvation	(Acts 4:12)
2. Justification	(Rom. 5:1)
3. Water Baptism	(Matt. 28:19)
4. Sanctification	(1 Thess. 4:3)
5. Baptism in the Holy Spirit	(Matt. 3:11)
6. Laying on of Hands	(Heb. 6:2)
7. Second Coming of Christ	(Acts 1:11)
8. The Resurrection of the Dead	(Heb. 6:2)
9. Judgment of the Righteous	(Rom. 14:10)
10. Judgment of the Unrighteous	(Rev. 20:11-15)
11. Eternal Life for the Righteous	(John 3:15)
12. Eternal Punishment for the Unrighteous	(Rev. 20:14)

The twelve gates on the first foundation are each made of one pearl (Rev. 21:21). In the New Testament, the pearl represents the preciousness of the Gospel. In the Kingdom parables, when a merchant was selling pearls and discovered one of great price, he sold all he had to purchase the valuable pearl (Matt. 13:45-46). The kingdom of heaven is like a *pearl of great price*. The pearl is mentioned again when Christ told His disciples not to give what was holy to the dogs, and never cast their pearls before swine (Matt. 7:6).

A natural pearl is created within an oyster when an intruder, such as a grain of sand, slips between the two shells of the oyster. As a defense mechanism, the oyster releases a mother-of-pearl substance called nacre, which creates a hard covering around the intruder and prevents the foreign substance from taking control of the oyster. This substance continues to be released until the intruder is completely covered and eventually, a beautiful pearl is formed.

Using the pearl analogy, the world encountered a spiritual intruder called Satan and his dark kingdom of rebellious spirits. The only way to defend themselves from these parasites was by a redemptive covenant through Christ, whose blood covers our sins, and the spiritual parasites are defeated. After adding many layers of Scripture and the cleansing power of Christ, a pearl of great price is created within us!

These gates of pearl are a reminder of the price that was paid to bring the Savior to the world to redeem mankind.

In the book of Revelation, John saw that the city was of pure gold (Rev. 21:18) and the street was transparent gold (Rev. 21:21). Ezekiel 28:13, after listing the nine stones, speaks of gold. One feature of the New Jerusalem is the massive amount of gold that is so pure it appears as transparent.

Gold must be purified by being melted at a temperature of around 1,945 degrees Fahrenheit. I was ministering in Irvine, Texas at a church pastored by Gary Meek, who had once been a successful jeweler in his community. He explained to me that, when gold is heated to the melting point, a jeweler will lower a graphite rod into the liquid gold, as the impurities in the liquid are pulled to the graphite like a magnet. Once the impurities are removed, the gold in the heated bowl forms a sheen on the surface that is so mirror-like, the jeweler can see his reflection on the surface. Whatever heat, fire and pressure were present in the early stages of creation caused the gold used in the building of the Holy City to change its molecular makeup to form gold, yet translucent streets.

GEMSTONES IN THE FOUNDATION WALLS

Notice that these same stones that are set on the breastplate of the High Priest (and the nine covering the anointed cherub) are also the same stones on the twelve different walls of the New Jerusalem! In Revelation we read:

> "And the foundations of the wall of the city were garnished with all manner of precious stones. The first foundation was jasper; the second, sapphire; the third, a chalcedony; the fourth, an emerald; The fifth, sardonyx; the sixth, sardius; the seventh, chrysolite; the eighth, beryl; the ninth, a topaz; the tenth, a chrysoprasus; the eleventh, a jacinth; the twelfth, an amethyst."
>
> – REV. 21:19-20

Here are the stones and each respective foundation of the Holy City, the New Jerusalem:

The Foundation Gemstone	The Foundation
Jasper	First foundation (21:19)
Sapphire	Second foundation (21:19)
Chalcedony (turquoise)	Third foundation (21:19)
Emerald	Fourth foundation (21:19)
Sardonyx (onyx)	Fifth foundation (21:20)
Sardius	Sixth foundation (21:20)
Chrysolite (diamond)	Seventh foundation (21:20)
Beryl	Eighth foundation (21:20)
Topaz	Ninth foundation (21:20)
Chrysoprase (agate)	Tenth foundation (21:20)
Ligure (Jacinth)	Eleventh foundation (21:20)
Amethyst	Twelfth foundation (21:20)

Now look again at the nine stones that formed the bright covering on the anointed cherub that would lead the rebellion in heaven, and compare them to the foundation levels and the tribal leaders:

Foundation of New Jerusalem	Stone on the Cherub	Son of Jacob it Represents
First foundation wall	Jasper	Benjamin
Second foundation wall	Sapphire	Simeon
Third foundation wall	Chalcedony	Levi
Fourth foundation wall	Emerald	Judah
Fifth foundation wall	Onyx	Joseph
Sixth foundation wall	Sardius	Reuben
Seventh foundation wall	Diamond	Naphtili
Eighth foundation wall	Beryl	Zebulun
Ninth foundation wall	Topaz	Simeon
Tenth foundation wall		Asher
Eleventh foundation wall		Gad
Twelfth foundation wall		Issachar

When comparing the nine gemstones covering the anointed cherub, with the stones in the walls of the New Jerusalem, something becomes obvious. He has no stones for the top three levels of the holy city—walls ten, eleven and twelve. The agate, the jacinth, and the amethyst are missing from the anointed cherub.

WHY ARE THREE STONES MISSING?

The mystery is why three gemstones are missing from the cherub's covering. Why did the High Priest have twelve and the cherub only nine? I believe there are two possible reasons.

When we observe the narrative of Jacob blessing his sons prior to his death, we see that these missing stones represent these three tribal fathers: Asher, Issachar, and Gad. Jacob predicted that *Asher* would bring forth royal dainties (Gen. 49:20); that *Issachar* would crouch between two burdens (Gen 49:14); and *Gad* would see a troop overcome him, but he would overcome in the end (Gen. 49:19). The summary of the three missing stones conceals this truth: Satan could never *produce a royal seed,* he could never *carry your burden,* and he would never *overcome in the end*!

The second reason for the missing stones is understood when we refer back to the "stones of fire." Notice this insight is penned twice in Ezekiel:

> "You were the anointed cherub who covers; I established you; you were on the holy mountain of God; you walked back and forth in the midst of fiery stones."
>
> – EZEK. 28:14

> "Therefore I cast you as a profane thing out of the mountain of God; and I destroyed you, O covering cherub, from the midst of the fiery stones."
>
> – EZEK. 28:16

The *mountain of God,* in both references, is the mountain in heaven where God is worshipped and where His original creative process of forming the heavens and earth originated. Just as the earthly Jerusalem in Israel was built upon a sacred mountain, identified as the *House of*

God and the *gate of heaven* (Gen. 28:17), this heavenly mountain is identified in Hebrews 12:22 and Revelation 14:1 as *Mount Sion*, the holy hill where angels worship and where the resurrected spirits of "just men made perfect" will dwell after the resurrection (Heb. 12:23).

The verse mentioned by Ezekiel about the *stones of fire* on the sacred mountain has been one of the most difficult to interpret. I have read countless commentaries and none have ever satisfied my curiosity or given me a clear understanding. Some scholars attribute this passage to a powerful king of Tyre and the stones of fire to the Phoenician glass industry, centered in the city of Tyre in Ezekiel's time.

However, to make this section of the prophecy apply to a human king is virtually impossible, as no human king would or could be identified as "the anointed cherub," and no Phoenician king was on the "mountain of God" and then cast out. This Ezekiel 28 reference alludes to a beautiful and stunning created cherub that was ranked superior to other angels and ministering sprits.

My discussion with Pastor Meeks sparked a fresh understanding for me on the subject of the stones of fire. I was questioning the mystery of the fiery stones on God's mountain when Gary said, "All gemstones found on the earth are formed by fire and great pressure."

The majority of earth's gemstones are found between 3 to 25 miles under the earth's crust. Some gemstones form in the earth's mantle, which consists primarily of hot molten rock called magma. When this magma slowly cools in the crust of the earth, it can crystalize and form minerals. As pressure builds, these crystals can enter rocks and form various types of gemstones. As rocks crack and the minerals and crystals enter the open spaces, veins of minerals can fill the cracks, forming a vein of stones. Most gemstone deposits on earth are located in and under mountains. In all cases, it requires intense heat, or fire, to cause the minerals to crystalize.

So what are the stones of fire? A Hebrew commentary published by A.S. Hartom (1953) of Umberto Cassuto's Masoretic text translates the stones of fire as sparkling stones—that is, gemstones which have been cut. Ezekiel 28:14 in the Cambridge Bible (1970) reads, "I will set you as a towering cherub as guardian; you were on God's holy hill and you walked proudly among the stones that flashed like fire." Thus it seems that these stones of fire were not burning rocks, but gemstones to be used for some purpose in heaven.

What was taking place in heaven in ages past that required the highest being among the angels, the anointed cherub, to walk among stones of fire? Notice the Bible does not speak of Satan walking *in fire*, but walking in the midst of the stones of fire. The word *stones* in Hebrew is *'eben* and comes from a root word meaning *to build*. Was something being *built from the stones of fire* on this holy mountain?

I believe these Ezekiel references are taking the reader back to the earliest ages of creation, when the heavens and earth were being formed by God, the sons of God were singing, and the morning stars were shouting for joy (Gen. 1:1; Job 38:4-7). In the beginning, after the creation of angels, I believe that an assignment was given to the chief angel to oversee the stones of fire—the gemstones that would be forged in heat and come forth in the form of beautiful and colorful crystals.

Then, at some point in the heavenly creation process, the New Jerusalem, the Holy City of God was created, layer by layer and wall upon wall, and studded with these colorful stones that had been forged in fire on the sacred mountain. The assignment to build the largest and most beautiful city in the cosmos was not only a significant mission to accomplish, but the *pride* concealed in one influential angel connected with the building assignment would seed a heavenly rebellion.

Ezekiel said that every precious stone was the covering of this magnificent angel (Ezek. 28:13). The word *covering* in Ezekiel 28:13 refers to an adornment of stone. Joseph wore a coat of many colors that identified him as his father's favorite son (Gen. 37:3), and this cherub wore a covering—not of cloth but of stones.

Consider the possibility that, working on this mountain, is a spirit being (Lucifer, the anointed cherub) whose very "body" is garnished with each stone that he creates for the New Jerusalem. Perhaps, when each level was completed, the reward for obedience and work was the gemstone for that foundation, either on a golden breastplate or layered like a stone-studded coat that covered his very being.

Ezekiel emphasized that God's cherub was "perfect in beauty" (28:12) and became lifted up (proud and arrogant) because of his beauty (28:12). When considering the brilliant colors of these flashing gemstones and how one angel was given access to God's secrets and His creative powers, then his beauty was not in the traditional sense of beauty—that is, beautiful eyes and skin, a handsome face, or lovely hair. His beauty was in his "covering."

When light hits a diamond at the right angle, it reflects a prism of many colors. Imagine, as the brightness of God's glory filled the heaven and light reflected on the cherub's covering of stones, the flashes of colorful light that must have illuminated off his body. No doubt the other angels were in awe of his beauty and shining glow. Iniquity found a seed in his own prideful perception of his beauty.

Based on the Ezekiel 28 list, his covering was limited to nine stones—the first nine gems from the stones of fire. But he was missing the last three that would complete the Holy City's twelve walls. Could this be a clue that Satan's rebellion and expulsion from heaven occurred in the midst of the building of the New Jerusalem, and the three gemstones missing from Lucifer indicate the timing of the rebellion—just after the ninth level of the Holy City was complete and before the tenth foundation was begun?

At some point, while Satan was walking in the stones of fire, he became proud of his beauty; and in Isaiah, we read that he desired to exalt his throne above the stars of God and make himself like God (Isa. 14:13-14). At that time in heaven, there was (and still is) a mountain of the congregation where God is worshipped, and Satan said he desired to sit in the mountain of the congregation (Isa. 14:13).

The Hebrew word for congregation is *mowed*, the word used in the Hebrew Scriptures for an appointment, a set time, or an assembly. It is the word used in the Torah when describing the seven feasts of Israel in Leviticus 23. The Hebrew word for feast is *mowed*, with the plural being *moadim*. These are holy convocations (Lev. 23:2), solemn feasts (Num. 15:3). Long before God established seven festivals for Israel, there were festival gatherings in heaven involving God and the angels!

There is a strong implication that Satan became lifted up in pride, because he wanted the city for himself and felt he deserved to be equal to or above God. With the stones missing on his breastplate, I believe this serves as a clue that he rebelled and was expelled before the city of God was complete—thus three stones are omitted from him.

If indeed, for every foundation completed, Satan was granted a gemstone covering, then he had nine and fell after the ninth foundation was completed. This means he was fired about three-fourths of the way through the building program.

This would explain why the beauty of this one-of-a-kind cherub, before his rebellion, was noted by the prophet Ezekiel. As the chief angel, he had influence over the sons of God and the morning star angels, and he himself was called the morning star or the son of the morning. Both groups of angelic camps observed God laying the foundation of the earth, and they rejoiced with Him. Remember, the earth was formed in ages past, before the total reformation and creation of life on earth, which began in Genesis 1:3.

All of this spiritual drama would have unfolded in ages past, before the creation of earth as we know it. Certain sons of God and morning star angels were so impressed with Satan's position, influence, beauty and ability, that when he made a decision to instigate a coup against the Creator, one third of the host of heaven believed he could be successful and were willing to join his rebellion. No doubt they were unaware that God's plan would be to hurl every one of them off the holy mountain!

Many of these same angels are the very ones who one day will battle Michael the archangel, who will conduct a second cosmic housecleaning and cast Satan and his hoards to the earth during the second half of the tribulation (Rev. 12:7-10). John saw Satan and his angels and Michael and his angels engaged in a celestial conflict, with Satan losing for a third time. He lost in ages past when he fell from heaven; he lost in ages present, when Christ defeated him on the cross, and he will lose in ages to come, as he will be cast down to the bottomless pit, then confined to the lake of fire!

SATAN'S HATRED FOR JERUSALEM

This could, at least in part, explain Satan's hatred for the city of Jerusalem. From a secular point of view, it makes no sense that so many wars have been fought over the city of Jerusalem, or that the city has changed hands more times and witnessed more bloodshed than just about any city in world history. Entire empires have fought over the city; and twice, under the Babylonians and the Romans, the Temple was seized and burned to the ground. Treasures were stolen and taken to the enemy's homelands.

The wealth of the Holy Temple was the motivation for both invasions. In the time of King Hezekiah, several Babylonians traveled to Jerusalem to visit the king, and during their tour Hezekiah showed them all the gold and silver vessels of the house of God. He hid nothing from them. After they left, Isaiah warned the king that he had unlocked the door of opportunity to a future invasion by the Babylonians—which did occur about 150 years later. The invasion was effective in seizing and transporting the treasures in Jerusalem to Babylon.

When the Jews returned from Babylon with a decree from Cyrus to rebuild the Temple and the city, the Samaritan leaders began a resistance campaign to stop the progress of the building program and discourage the Jews from completing their assignment.

Then there were the Romans. Imperial Rome faced enormous debts, especially from paying for a massive army to keep peace in occupied lands—including Israel. The Jewish rebellion against the Romans gave the emperor and his legions a reason to invade Jerusalem, where they took loads of valuable treasure back to Rome.

While this may explain the reason for two empires seeking wealth, it cannot explain why Jerusalem has been invaded, destroyed and rebuilt so many times. Neither does it explain the hatred that the Jews and Israel have experienced for centuries, or for that matter the ongoing conflict between Judaism and Islam. There is an invisible force motivating world leaders and armies to erase the existence of Jerusalem from the world scene and, once and for all, rid the planet of this sacred city.

I suggest to you that God's first created angel was the morning star—the cherub also known in the King James Translation as Lucifer. God established the law of the first—the first fruits and the firstborn. The firstborn Jewish son received a double blessing of the Father's birthright—meaning that when the father of the family passed, the older son inherited twice as much, as he was considered his father's strength.

The tabernacle was a reflection of the heavenly temple, and the earthly Jerusalem was a reflection of the heavenly Jerusalem. When Satan and his angels hear the name "Jerusalem," imagine the wrath he releases toward the city where God put His name (Deut. 12:21)!

THE TWELVE STONES FOUND ON EARTH

When Pastor Gary Meek and I discussed how gemstones were created in the earth, we talked about how different types of stones are found on different continents on the earth. For example, a tanzanite is found in Tanzania, Africa, as the majority of world's tanzanite mines are there. Diamonds are found in various nations, but the best come from Africa. The best quality emeralds are mined in South America.

Each precious gemstone in the twelve walls of the 1500-mile-high New Jerusalem is found somewhere on earth in different locations. While gemstones are created throughout the earth, some nations are known for mining particular gems:

Sardis	Siberia, Germany, India, Brazil
Topaz	Africa, China, Japan, United States, Pakistan
Emerald	Brazil, Columbia, Pakistan, Zambia, Russia
Chalcedony (Turquoise)	Iran, Israel, Mexico, China, America, Pakistan
Sapphire	Myanmar, India, Sri Lanka, Thailand, Kenya
Diamond	South Africa, Canada, Australia
Onyx	Brazil, Madagascar, India
Jasper	Spain, Madagascar, America
Beryl	America, Russia, Brazil
Jacinth	Africa, Vietnam, Australia, India, Brazil, America

Agate	Mexico, China, America, Argentina
Amethyst	America, Russia, Sri Lanka, Brazil

On earth, the stones found on God's heavenly city are found in nations of many tribes and ethnic groups. The Holy City New Jerusalem will become the eternal dwelling for people from "every kindred, tongue and people" (Rev. 5:9). These twelve gems that layer the outer walls of the massive city of God were formed in the same manner that precious metals and gems are formed in the earth—in fire and heat.

We don't think of heaven as a place where fire is a prominent manifestation. However, when God descended on Mount Sinai we read:

> "Now Mount Sinai was completely in smoke, because the Lord descended upon it in fire. Its smoke ascended like the smoke of a furnace, and the whole mountain quaked greatly."
>
> – EXODUS 19:18

For forty years while Israel journeyed, the Lord manifested in a column of fire by night (Exod. 13:21). The intense heat and radiation emitting from stars, and the mixture of cosmic gases that create the appearance of lights in the heaven, reveal that *fire and heat* were all part of the early creative process of heaven and earth. Scientists are steadfast in their belief that the earth was once a ball of molten fire. In the beginning, God created the heaven and the earth (Genesis 1:1). In Genesis 1:2, the earth was void and without form, with no life anywhere on the planet. The light of God (Gen. 1:3) and the sun enabled the earth to sustain the life God would speak into existence.

Creationists often reject the scientific idea that the earth was once a molten ball of fire. However, this planet was created "in the beginning," and nobody actually knows how long ago that was. We know that angels were created long before Adam, but how long before, we do not know. I personally believe there is a gap of time between Genesis 1:1 and 1:2. Hell was prepared for the devil and his angels, and these beings were already fallen before the creation of Adam. Since hell, Biblically, is located in the bowels of the earth, it is possible that the earth was originally a fire ball, and eventually was cooled by water as recorded in Genesis 1:2. This water would have provided a cooling effect in preparation for God to separate the dry land from the watery sea.

When astronomers peer through multi-million dollar telescopes into deep space, they can view heavenly lights and nebulas that are impossible to see with normal eyesight. From our visual spectrum, the night stars are like pinpoints of light scattered on a massive blanket of darkness. We see tiny bright specks randomly dotting one end of heaven to the other. Once we enter the heart of the universe, a new and different imagery emerges. The solid black curtain becomes millions of nebulas with gases of green, yellow, orange, blue and red. These colorful pockets of gas, stars and cosmic dust are layered throughout the measureless universe.

From earth's view, all mankind sees is a blue sky in the day and a black heaven at night. Yet, the further you travel into the galaxy, that black atmosphere becomes filled with colors, unseen to the human eye without advanced telescopes. When looking through the lens of NASA's Hubble Telescope, one can only imagine what we have not yet seen that is millions of light years away, in the land of the original mountain of fire.

CHAPTER 6

Two Powerful Angels
Expelled with Satan

IN AGES PAST, when Satan was hurled off God's sacred mountain, a third of the angels were expelled with him (Rev. 12:4). In the kingdom of darkness, there are numerous evil and unclean spirits named in the Bible, including a spirit of *bondage* (Rom. 8:15), a spirit of *heaviness* (Isa. 61:3), a *lying* spirit (1 Kings 22:23), a *tormenting* spirit (1 John 4:18), a spirit of *fear* (2 Tim. 1:7), a spirit of *infirmity* (Luke 13:11) and a spirit of *jealousy* (Num. 5:14), just to name a few.

These various types of spirits are demonic entities assigned to attack individuals. However, the stronger *prince* spirits, called principalities (Eph. 6:12), are higher ranking fallen angels that were part of God's original "sons of God" and "morning stars" group (Job 38:7), who were deceived into following Satan in his prideful rebellion.

Scripture identifies three fallen angels by name, two being the prince of *Persia* (Dan. 10:13) and the prince of *Greece* (Dan. 10:20). Both are chief prince spirits ruling over the upper cosmic realm above Persia and Greece, and they influence Grecian and Persian national leaders to invoke negative legislation or influence in their decisions against the Jews and Israel. The third fallen angel is Abaddon or Apollyon (Rev. 9:11), identified as the king angel over the bottomless pit.

However, many believers are unaware that *death* is not just a word for the end of life, nor is *hell* just the name of a fiery chamber located under the earth. Death and Hell are literally *two powerful fallen angels*.

In the New Testament, the English word *hell* in the Greek is *hades*; it is used ten times (Matt. 11:23; 16:18; Luke 10:15; 16:23; Acts 2:27, 31; Rev. 1:18; 6:8; 20:13, 14). John reveals in Revelation that both death and hell are spirit beings:

> "So I looked, and behold, a pale horse. And the name of him who sat on it was Death, and Hades followed with him. And power was given to them over a fourth of the earth, to kill with sword, with hunger, with death, and by the beasts of the earth."
>
> – REVELATION 6:8

When we think of death, we think of the cessation of life, when the heart stops beating and the person stops breathing, then moments later is pronounced clinically dead. In Scripture, the act of dying occurs when the soul and spirit is separated from the physical body (see Luke 16:19-31; 2 Cor. 5:6), and the eternal spirit is removed and carried to either paradise (if the person was in covenant with God) or to hell (if the person was wicked). Through Adam's sin in the Garden of Eden, death entered the world (Rom. 5:12) and all men are now subject to experience physical death (Heb. 9:27).

In Exodus 12, a *death angel* (called the destroyer, Exodus 12:23) passed through Egypt and snuffed out the lives of all firstborn not under the protective covering of the lamb's blood. Not only is death an enemy of God and the last enemy to be destroyed (1 Cor. 15:25-26), but after the great white throne judgment, both death and hell are forever confined in the lake of fire:

> "Then Death and Hades were cast into the lake of fire. This is the second death."
>
> – REVELATION 20:14

If Death and Hades were something other than actual spirit beings, they could not be confined eternally in the lake of fire. Death is described as riding on a *pale* horse. The Greek word *pale* in Revelation 6:8 is *chloros*, a word which literally translated means *green*; thus the color of death is a sickly, pale green.

Hades, the Greek word for hell, has an interesting history among the Greeks. They believed that Hades was a god who was lord over the spirits of the underworld. Jesus spoke of the gates of hell not prevailing against the church, and He used the Greek word *hades* (Matt. 16:18). He was saying that the spirits, strategies, and powers of the invisible satanic world, including the spirits of death and hell, would never prevail against Christ's church! After Christ was raised from the dead, He declared that He alone possesses the keys (authority) over death and hell (Rev. 1:18).

WHERE DID DEATH ORIGINATE?

I always believed that death originated on earth with Adam and Eve in the garden, after they sinned by partaking of the tree of knowledge of good and evil, and was simply a natural process at the end of the human life cycle. However, if death is a fallen angel, then both *Death* and *Hades* were originally angels created by God. They were, in ages past, angelic hosts on the mountain of God with the anointed cherub, and were part of the sons of God and morning stars, and their original assignments were within the celestial kingdom.

In ages past, when the angel Satan walked on the stones of fire, he did not have the name Satan, the devil, or the dragon. These are all present names that represent his evil and seductive nature (Rev. 12:9). His two names mentioned before his fall were simply "son of the morning" (Isaiah 14:12) and "the anointed cherub" (Ezekiel 28:14). In ages past, death, and hell were not the names of these angels, but all things changed after the rebellion on the mountain.

The Bible teaches that, when Satan was expelled from heaven, the everlasting fire (of hell) was prepared for the devil and his angels (Matt. 25:41). This fiery chamber is under the earth's crust, as hell is always referred to as being down and never up (Ps. 55:15; Pr. 7:27; 15:24; Isa. 14:9; Ezek. 31:16). The devil's angels ("his angels" - Matt. 25:41) refer to *fallen angels*, including many of the most wicked ones that are presently bound in chains of darkness in a deep, underworld chamber that, in Greek, is called *tartarus*. This is translated as hell in the English version of the Bible (see 2 Peter 2:4 and Jude 6), and it is the lowest part of hell where the worst spirits are confined. This fiery section of hell is presently burning deep under the foundations of the mountains. God spoke to Moses saying:

> "For a fire is kindled in My anger, and shall burn to the lowest hell; It shall consume the earth with her increase, and set on fire the foundations of the mountains."
>
> – DEUTERONOMY 32:22 (NKJV)

When the prophet Jonah was drowning in the sea, he mentioned the mountain. He described the sensation of seaweeds wrapping around his head (Jon. 2:5) and recalled his memory of slowly dying as his soul fainted within him. Jonah recalled:

> "I went down to the moorings of the mountains; the earth with its bars closed behind me forever; Yet You have brought up my life from the pit."
>
> – JONAH 2:6 (NKJV)

Jonah actually died and the great fish swallowed him, which helped preserve his body for a later resurrection. Jonah's spirit descended into the underworld and was bought back into his body three days later—a literal resurrection from the dead!

There are fallen angels now reserved in chains in the *tartarus* compartment, to be brought out from the netherworld of the dead and fallen angels, and to be judged at the great white throne judgment (2 Pet. 2:4). A large number of these fallen angels are a remnant of the "sons of God," who were the angels that descended to earth, took on the form of men, had relations with the daughters of men, and birthed a race of giants, referred to in Genesis 6:1-4 (This is taught in detail on my DVD titled, *Fallen Angels, Giants and Evil Spirits.)*

I am uncertain of the original names of the two fallen angels we now call *death* and *hell*. It is also unclear what position they might have held in the pre-Adamic creation. But these are two of the strongest and most powerful team members in Satan's kingdom. Together with Satan, Death and Hell (hades) make a fearsome threesome in the battle for the souls of mankind.

In Scripture, spiritual authority is often manifest in threes: Father,

Son and Holy Spirit; Abraham, Isaac and Jacob; body, soul, and spirit; outer court, inner court and Holy of Holies. During the tribulation, the beast, the antichrist and false prophet form a satanic triangle of death, darkness and destruction. Since Satan fell, he, death, and hell are the triple threat to humanity.

THE SEPARATION IN HEAVEN

Physical death occurs when the human spirit is separated from the body, for the "body without the spirit is dead" (James 2:26). In ages past, when Satan's angelic rebellion occurred and a third of the angels were cast out of heaven with him, is it possible that this *separation of created spirits* from God's presence initiated, not a physical death, since angels are not physical beings, but a "spirit" of death, as this expulsion was a separation of rebellious spirits from the rest of God's created angels?

The Genesis narrative reveals the releasing of the spirit of death upon mankind. In the Garden of Eden, God warned man not to eat from the tree of knowledge of good and evil, because if he did, in the *day* that he ate, he would die (Gen. 2:17). Yet, when Adam and Eve ate from the tree, they did not immediately die *that day*, or at least not physically. Adam lived hundreds of additional years, eventually dying at 930 years of age. Adam's death that day was an *internal spiritual death* and a separation of Adam's *spiritual nature* from the *nature of God*.

The *spiritual death* was followed hundreds of years later by Adam's *physical* death.

Sin paved the road that death and hell rode upon to enter the earth's realm. While death is a natural process that creeps toward us as we age and brings all under its cold grip, the overseer of death is the angel of death himself. The difference between the physical death of a believer and a sinner is that, for a believer, the sting of death has been removed, and the final victory ticket that death would claim is void when a believer passes. The believer's song is, "Grave where is thy victory, death where is thy sting" (1 Cor. 15:55)?

THE SHADOW OF DEATH

Eighteen times in seventeen verses the phrase "shadow of death" is mentioned. *Shadow of death* is two Hebrew words, *tsêl* (shadow) and *mawet* (death). In the twenty-third Psalm, David speaks of walking through the "valley of the shadow of death" (Psalms 23:4).

What is death's shadow? Picture a six-foot, five-inch boxer with two boxing gloves covering his hands. Bright lights expose his bulging muscles, and perspiration drips from his face and stubby beard. On the concrete floor is a black shadow, giving a darkened image of the real person. Would the *boxer* or the *shadow* be your greatest threat? The boxer, of course. A shadow cannot harm anyone. It may reflect the image of a strong body, but all the wild air punches will never land on anyone, as you watch the shadow of a boxer beat his way to an imaginary victory.

Satan, Death and Hell are fallen spirits, and are feared and dreaded by those who are familiar with their methods that lead to eternal separation from God. Death is real, but for a believer in covenant with God, death is only a shadow, with no authority to defeat and proclaim a final victory when a believer dies. Our departure from earth to heaven is so swift, that by the time death blinks we have exited this life and entered into the next.

It is appointed for all men once to die, followed by the judgment (Heb. 9:27). Yet, when the hoof beats of the pale horse and rider strike the ground, heading toward a believer's front door, the Christ-follower will encounter only the shadow of death, in which there is no fear. Even the sting of death has been removed through Christ's death and resurrection. A shadow cannot produce death and sorrow for the redeemed; death is only a release from the body that returns to dust.

In ages past, when the angelic host worshipped in the mountain of God and when there was not yet an introduction of sin on earth, *there was no angel of death or hell* released upon the planet. And in the end, God will expel death and hell forever from the presence of His resurrected family (Rev. 21:4).

Who were the spirits of death and hell in ages past before the fall of Satan? That remains a mystery. However, both were significant enough that, when Satan made claim to mankind in the garden, sin blasted open gates that enabled two of the most fierce and destructive spirits to influence the lifespan of humanity and, for some, their eternal destination.

Christ now holds in His possession the keys (authority) over death and hell. A believer should never fear that Satan has the authority to take your life. If he had this power, he would have used it long before you were converted. Christ not only has authority over death and hell, but he controls your time of departure from earth and possesses the key to heaven's door, which opens for you when you arrive.

In Luke 16, when the beggar died, angels (plural) carried his spirit into the next life. We assume there were two angels involved in this transition. Satan's two afterlife agents are *death and hell;* but for a believer, death and hell are conquered by God's angels, who escort a believer into the world to come.

CHAPTER 7

When Saints Judge the Angels

THE APOSTLE PAUL wrote to the church in Corinth, Greece, which was a congregation experiencing strife and division among its membership and advised them not to take other believers to a secular court to be judged by an unbelieving judge:

> "Dare any of you, having a matter against another, go to law before the unrighteous, and not before the saints? Do you not know that the saints will judge the world? And if the world will be judged by you, are you unworthy to judge the smallest matters? Do you not know that we shall judge angels?"
>
> – 1 CORINTHIANS 6:1-3 (NJKV)

Paul admonished believers to handle such matters within the church itself, with the final decision being determined by spiritual leadership. He reminded the church of two astonishing facts: Believers will one day judge the *world* and also judge the *angels*.

The judgment of the world and the angels has been set for an appointed time: immediately following the one-thousand-year reign of Christ on earth. All sinners, from the beginning of creation to the moment of this judgment, will face a judgment at what scholars identify as the great white throne judgment. John saw this final judgment in his Patmos vision when he wrote:

> "Then I saw a great white throne and Him who sat on it, from whose face the earth and the heaven fled away. And there was found no place for them. And I saw the dead, small and great,

standing before God, and books were opened. And another book was opened, which is the book of Life. And the dead were judged according to their works, by the things which were written in the books. The sea gave up the dead who were in it, and Death and Hades delivered up the dead who were in them. And they were judged, each one according to his works. Then Death and Hades were cast into the lake of fire. This is the second death. And anyone not found written in the Book of Life was cast into the lake of fire."

– REVELATION 20:11-15

Notice that Death and Hades give up the dead. These dead are the souls and spirits of the unrighteous who died throughout the ages and were confined until this judgment. For example, this would include all sinners from the time of Adam's descendants to the very end of the millennial reign of Christ. It would include the rich man mentioned in Luke 16, who was confined in hell because he trusted in his riches and refused to feed a sickly beggar named Lazarus (Luke 16:19-31).

Christ gave a stunning preview of this judgment when He spoke of a group of men and one woman who would condemn the multitudes of his generation. Christ said the men of Nineveh and the Queen of the South (the Queen of Sheba) would raise up and condemn those who rejected Christ, after seeing His miracles and remaining in unbelief (see Matthew 12:41-42).

Christ also mentioned those who lived in the city of Sodom. This was a wicked and perverse city which Lot, his wife, and two daughters fled from when God rained fire from heaven and destroyed four of the five cities in the southern plains of the Dead Sea. Thousands were burned alive and only four escaped, with Lot's wife looking back and experiencing judgment (see Genesis 19). Christ warned His generation of unbelieving religious leaders that, at the judgment, it would be better to be a man from Sodom standing before God being judged than for one of them to be judged on that day. Perhaps this is because Sodom had no Bibles, no prophets, and no one preaching to them before they perished.

Christ's generation, however, had the Messiah, the Apostles, and the miracles; yet they continued in their unbelief. Where much is given, much will be required (Luke 12:48). Those with knowledge of the truth who rejected the truth will receive greater punishment than those who knew little or nothing. This is why Christ warned the Pharisees that in hell they would receive "greater damnation" (Matt. 23:14; Mark 12:40; Luke 20:47). The Greek word *damnation* is *krima* and, in the context of Christ's warning, refers to a final decision made in a court that condemns a person as guilty.

The judgment of the entire world of sinners, unbelievers, Christ mockers, shedders of innocent blood, and the unrighteous will stand at the great white throne of God and know in detail why they are being condemned. After all, this is a judgment in which a person is able to present their case and their cause before the judge.

There are books in heaven that reveal the words and deeds of each person who has ever lived, and these books don't lie. Any statements that contradict these books will not stand in the heavenly court. Perhaps there are a multitude of people in hell who do not know why God released their spirit to this fiery underworld, and why they were not permitted to enter the kingdom of heaven. To illustrate this, Christ said that not everyone who calls him Lord will enter the kingdom, but only those who do the will of God. He described moments in this judgment when men would claim to have cast out devils, healed the sick, prophesied, and done great works, yet they practiced lawlessness and had no true intimate relationship with Christ (Matt. 7:22-23).

How will these individuals be judged? Those who lived before the Law of Moses (Adam to Moses) and who lived under the Law (Moses to Christ) would have to be judged by their knowledge and understanding from their own era. This may be why there are twenty-four elders, twelve being the sons of Jacob, who would judge those from the Old Testament era by their spiritual understanding and the Laws of God.

In the underground chambers of hell, and in the area that was once known as Abraham's bosom, Abraham told the rich man that those living on the earth have Moses and the prophets; let them hear them (Luke 16:29). The rich man was convinced that his five living brothers could be converted if a man returned from the dead to warn them about hell. Abraham refuted this statement, saying that if they don't believe the Law and prophets, they will not believe an amazing sign, such as a resurrection from the dead.

This fact is observed in Christ's ministry, when He raised the dead and still some refuted the miracle and refused to believe (John 12:9-10).

For those living from the time of the resurrection to the end of the one-thousand-year reign of Christ, the Scriptures themselves will testify against them at this judgment. Paul said that both believers and unbelievers will be judged by the writing of the Scripture—by God's Divine revelation of the New Covenant that provides eternal life to all who believe upon Christ, repent, and follow Him. Paul wrote, "In the day when God will judge the secrets of men by Jesus Christ, according to my gospel" (Rom. 2:16).

JUDGING THE ANGELS

Speaking by Divine revelation, Paul wrote that the saints will judge the angels. The only heavenly judgment in which this can occur would be at the Great White Throne judgment. Satan will be bound for one thousand years in the abyss, a dark endless pit, and at the conclusion of the thousand years, he will be loosed, along with the other demonic spirits, to lead a final military-style rebellion against Christ and the saints. He and his rebels will be defeated, and the heavenly judgment will follow this rebellion (see Revelation 20:7-15). Following the angelic judgment, Satan will be thrown into the lake of fire for eternity, where he will be tormented day and night forever and ever (Rev. 20:10).

In the judgment of the angels, there are two classifications of angels: the *faithful* and the *fallen*. The faithful are the angels who refused to follow Satan in his rebellion against God, and the fallen are those who chose to align themselves with Satan (Lucifer), believing he would somehow overthrow the throne of God and seize control of the heavenly temple and the worship of the angels.

It seems unlikely the saints will judge the *faithful angels*, as they remained obedient to God and have followed the Lord's instruction in detail from the pre-creation of Adam to the moment of the white throne judgment. Two of the Bible's noted and loyal followers of the Almighty are the angel Gabriel (Dan. 8:16; 9:21; Luke 1:19, 26) and the archangel Michael (Dan. 10:13, 21; 12:1; Jude 9; Rev. 12:7).

Gabriel served God as a special messenger, and brought God's revelation to Daniel, Zacharias, and Mary (mother of Jesus). Michael is the warring angel that God assigns during prophetic seasons to deal directly with Satan and his high level agents, taking them on in face-to-face combat in the heavenly realm (see Daniel 10; Rev. 12:7-10).

The New Testament is clear, however, that the fallen angels (whose actual numbers are unknown) are being reserved in chains under the earth for the day they will be judged. We read:

> "And the angels who did not keep their proper domain, but left their own abode, He has reserved in everlasting chains under darkness for the judgment of the great day: as Sodom and Gomorrah, and the cities around them in a similar manner to these, having given themselves over to sexual immorality and gone after strange flesh, are set forth as an example, suffering the vengeance of eternal fire."
>
> – JUDE 6-7 (NKJV)

> "For if God did not spare the angels who sinned, but cast them down to hell and delivered them into chains of darkness, to be reserved for judgment..."
>
> – 2 PETER 2:4-5 (NKJV)

These are the *fallen class of angels* that were linked, as previously mentioned, to the "sons of God" who came into the daughters of men and created a race of pre-flood and post-flood giants on the earth. Job said that God charged these angels with folly (Job 4:18). The Hebrew word *folly* is *toholah*, and can refer to someone who "makes great boasting or bragging upon themselves." In context, it could refer to Satan boasting that he would exalt his throne above the stars of God's and be like the Most High (Isa. 14:12-15).

Giants roamed the earth both before and after Noah's flood. Eventually, the last of the four giants remaining on the earth were slain by David's mighty men about three thousand years ago (2 Sam.

21:15-22). At some point, to prevent this mixing of the seed to continue on earth, God seized the angels that were assigned to earth and bound them in darkness under the earth. Peter wrote that they were "cast down to hell" (2 Pet. 2:4-5).

The word hell is found twenty-three times in the New Testament. Twelve times the Greek word translated hell is *gehenna* (Hebrew: Ge-Hinnom, see Matt. 5:22, 29, 30 10:28, etc.). Ten times in the New Testament the Greek word for hell is *haides* (hades), which among the Greeks was said to be a chamber that housed departed souls under the earth (Matt. 11:23; 16:18; Luke 10:15; Acts 2:27 etc.). When Peter identified the prison of these fallen angels as hell, he used a Greek word found only once in the New Testament—*tartaroo*, known as tartarus.

Long before Peter's statement, the Greeks had developed an elaborate mythology about the underworld, including hades (the realm of the dead) and tartarus, a region that lay under the earth far below hades. It was believed to be the deepest of two parts of the underworld, where the gods confined their enemies.

Obviously, since the Bible is inspired of God, there is, indeed, such a massive chamber under the earth that bears the name tartarus, where fallen angels and reproducers of the race of giants are bound in darkness, awaiting the judgment. In Greek mythology, the place is surrounded by a bronze wall and a set of gates, and is guarded by the hundred-handed giants.

The Greek poets Homer and Hesiod wrote of tartarus being a huge cosmic pit underneath the earth, located far beneath hades. The Greeks were known to embellish actual narratives in history and place their own gods as the warriors in great cosmic and earthly battles. The Bible, however, is not a book of myths but of facts and truth. Both Jude and Peter allude to angels being confined in chains of darkness (2 Pet. 2:4) and under darkness (Jude 6). During the thousand years of Christ's rule, Satan will be confined in chains to prevent him from escaping his prison. I am uncertain of what these chains are that could restrain spirit beings. However, these angels are being held until the moment of judgment.

John revealed that, just prior to the white throne judgment, hell will deliver up the dead that are in them (Rev. 20:13). At this final judgment, the entire underworld will be emptied of every spirit it holds—the sinners and the fallen angels—and all will stand before God and receive the final verdict. The saints of all ages will judge the world and the angels. The world will be judged by the law and the covenants, but how can a fallen angel be judged? Obviously, only God and His angels were present to see, hear, and experience the massive attempted overthrow of God's Divine system and position, by one rebellious cherub and his followers. All we know of this narrative is what is found in the Scriptures.

We know there is detailed information recorded in heavenly books of the words, deeds, and actions of every living person. Perhaps the ancient books record the details of these angels and will be read before the heavenly assembly of saints, and we will judge the activities of the fallen angels from the time they were expelled until they were confined. Others speculate that God has the ability to replay the events of history before the heavenly court, where they can observe first hand their words and actions (although this is speculation and not found in Scripture). The Bible mentions that books are opened which reveal the details (Rev. 20:12).

RULING OVER THE ANGELS

In Hebrews chapter one, the writer expounds on the fact that the Messiah (Christ) is greater than the angels. In chapter two he ponders man's spiritual authority, which was "a little lower than the angels" (Heb. 2:7). Then the writer speaks of the world to come, which in most cases refers not to the millennial reign of Christ, but to eternity, when all enemies are under Christ's feet, when death has been banished, and when the New Jerusalem descends upon a new earth (Rev. 21:1-2).

Of this time, Paul reveals:

> "For He has not put the world to come, of which we speak, in subjection to angels. But one testified in a certain place, saying:
>
> "What is man that You are mindful of him,
> Or the son of man that You take care of him?
> You have made him a little lower than the angels;
> You have crowned him with glory and honor,
> And set him over the works of Your hands.
> You have put all things in subjection under his feet."
>
> – HEBREWS 2:5-8 (NKJV)

While Paul's statement here speaks of Christ becoming a man (lower than the angels) and receiving glory through His defeat of His enemies, note that the world to come will not be under the subjection of the angels. It will, however, be the resurrected saints, the righteous ones from all ages, who will be given a kingdom and a dominion that will never end (Dan. 7:27).

When exploring the Apocalypse and reading the final two chapters, John's dynamic vision details the world to come, when at the conclusion of the great white throne judgment, God will purge the heavens and earth with a burning fire (2 Pet. 3:12-13) and will form a renewed planet with a renewed heaven, identified as the "new heaven and the new earth" (Isa 65:17; Rev. 21:1). The faithful angels will continue their activities in heaven. However, on the new earth, the saints will have complete dominion.

At that time, eternity will be only beginning. Much will be missing in the world to come that was common in the previous life. There is no more sin, death, crying, sorrow, or pain (Rev. 21:4). With the banishing of Satan, the fallen angels, all demonic powers, and wicked men, there will be no need for the continuous ministry of angels as we have known in this life. God does not give angels subjection (control) in the world to come, but He gives control to the overcoming saints who were promised they could eat from the tree of life (Rev. 2:7), be given power over the nations (Rev. 2:26), and be given the blessing of abiding in the New Jerusalem (Rev. 3:12).

One of the most powerful blessings to the overcomer is found in Revelation 3:12. When I was about twelve years of age, a member of my father's church had access to secure areas of the Pentagon. He took Dad, my brother, and me on a tour of this important federal institution where world-changing decisions were made. I recall entering the office of a renowned military person whose name was occasionally spoken on the national news. He was not in his office, but Dad's friend said, "Go ahead and sit in his chair. Just don't touch anything on the desk." As a young boy, I was in awe to know I was sitting in the chair of this famous man.

Yet, in Revelation 3:12, Christ promised the overcomer—those who remain loyal and faithful until the end—that they would sit upon His throne. The stipulation is for Christ's followers to be faithful unto death or faithful unto His return, whichever comes first.

SATAN MUST FACE HIS OWN JUDGMENT

Since we are judging the angels and Satan is a fallen cherub, it stands to reason that Satan will be present to face his own judgment. If and when Satan stands before his Creator God and attempts to present some form of defense to prevent his final doom in the lake of fire, what might Satan present to defend his early rebellion?

Satan's present position is accuser of the believers (Rev. 12:10), so what crafty accusations could be hurled against God? He cannot attack God's love, for His love is everlasting (Rom. 8:35); neither can he assault God's mercy, as His mercy endures forever (Psa. 107:1). He cannot accuse God of being unfaithful, as He is faithful that promised (Heb. 10:23). He cannot find one lie God has ever told since "God cannot lie" (Titus 1:2). Satan has no charge against God being a sinner, since He has never sinned, and he has no accusation against God as unrighteous, since He is a righteous judge (2 Tim. 4:8).

No accusation against God can stick, so what might his next strategy in the court of heaven be to defend himself? Can you image Satan saying, "I was your favorite angel, covered with precious stones and radiating your glory, and you became jealous of my beauty and kicked me out." Can you image God's response, as He turns to a city that is 1500 miles across and high, garnished with twelve different stones and replies, "So you want to talk about something beautiful? Just look at heaven! What are you compared to that?"

Perhaps he could use this defense: "You expelled me and never gave me an opportunity to repent as you gave Adam. This is not true justice!" The fact is, Satan could never repent, nor would he be permitted to, as his sin was equal to blasphemy, which cannot be forgiven in this life nor the life the come (Mark 3:28-29).

The adversary is a deceiver and a liar, and I have imagined the accusations he would throw at God in his attempt to expose the entire plan of redemption as a farce that was propagated against mankind. Perhaps his final plea would be, "The so-called act of redemption never occurred. The multitudes believed a lie and Christ was never crucified!" The theory that Christ was never crucified is believed by all Muslims in the world, who accept that Christ was a prophet, but do not believe He was the Son of God crucified.

Should this false charge be made before the heavenly court, the mouth of the adversary will be forever shut when Christ the Redeemer steps forward and exposes the scars in His hands and feet from the nails that held Him to the cross. Redemption was sealed, case closed. Satan will be condemned for eternity. His own choices set his destiny and his actions sealed his doom.

I believe there is something of great importance concealed in this judgment that is often overlooked. I am certain there are a multitude of individuals who stepped into eternity, thinking they had secured a spot in heaven, only to discover seconds after departing their physical bodies that their road of life ended at a cavern of darkness or a pit of fire. Some placed their confidence in their good works, or in their church doctrine that guaranteed that if they remained a member of some historical denomination, their activities in life had no bearing on their eternal destiny. Others believe that, if they go to hell, enough prayers and offerings to the church will release them from their temporary place of torment.

Consider also the thousands of terrorists who were convinced by their imams in the mosques that, if they would only strap a bomb to their bodies and detonate it, killing infidels in the process, they would enter paradise where seventy-two virgins will greet them and give them pleasure for eternity. As their bodies were blown to bits, their spirits awoke—not with seventy-two virgins, but perhaps with seventy-two demons—tormenting them. No doubt each of these individuals now understands why they missed the kingdom of the one true and living God.

However, just in case someone wonders why they were imprisoned in this underworld, God will host a universal judgment of all people from all nations throughout history, and reveal to them their sins as recorded in the heavenly books. They will be faced with their pride, rebellion, rejection of the Gospel and wicked deeds, and they will know why they will be separated from the righteous.

Hell was not originally created for human beings who were formed in the image of God; hell was created for the devil and his angels (Matt. 25:41). However, after the spiritual collapse in Eden, every person could choose to serve one of two masters: either God or the devil. Jesus understood this when He told the hypocritical Pharisees, *"You are of your father the devil and the lust of your father you will do..."* (John 8:44). If men choose to reject God's love, mercy and forgiveness, and if they choose to walk in their pride and rebellion, they choose their own spiritual father and will spend eternity with that particular father—whom Jesus warned was the devil. He said it this way:

> "And I say to you that many will come from the east and west, and sit down with Abraham, Isaac, and Jacob in the kingdom of heaven. But the sons of the kingdom will be cast out into outer darkness. There will be weeping and gnashing of teeth."
>
> – MATTHEW 8:11-12

It may seem odd to "judge the angels," as these fallen beings certainly already know their doom is set and their final destiny sealed. This is evident when Christ expelled demons from the man of Gadera. The chief demon petitioned Christ not to "send them into the deep" (Luke 8:31 KJV). The Greek word here for *deep* is *abussos*, and is translated in the book of Revelation as bottomless pit (Rev. 9:1, 2, 11; 11:7; 17:8), the same pit where Satan will be confined for a thousand years.

This one statement in Luke 8:31 indicates that the evil spirits under Satan's domain will also be sent into the abyss when Satan is seized at the conclusion of the tribulation and before the reign of Christ begins on earth (Rev.20:1-3).

Matthew also records the same narrative found in Luke of the man possessed with thousands of demons, and noted where the demons said to Christ, "Are you come to torment us before the time?" (Matt. 8:29). Thus fallen angels, demons, all of Satan's spirit rebels, already know their destiny is irreversible. Even in the middle of the seven-year tribulation, Satan will invade the earth, knowing he has but a short time (Rev. 12:12). So why spend time at a judgment, judging a host of angelic and spirit rebels who are already headed to the lake of fire?

One simple answer to this question may be found in a Genesis narrative. God was preparing to destroy Sodom and Gomorrah, when He delayed the judgment by sending angels to inform Abraham and warn Lot, thus giving him an opportunity to escape the coming judgment. Abraham negotiated with God and requested that Sodom be spared if ten righteous could be found. Abraham won the negotiation with this statement, "Shall not the Judge of the earth do right?"

Solomon wrote that God "shall judge the righteous and the wicked" (Eccl. 3:17). All created beings, those who have transgressed the law, deserve a judgment before a final sentencing. This is the right thing to do.

CHAPTER 8

The New Jerusalem:
Cube or Pyramid?

T HE MASSIVE HOLY City called New Jerusalem is assumed to be a giant *cube* that is 1,500 miles in width, length and height. Besides having a wall of twelve colorful gemstones, the beautiful city has twelve gates—three at each cardinal entrance—each made of a solid pearl and guarded by twelve angels. The names of the twelve tribes of Israel are carved on the twelve gates.

All of this information is confirmed in Revelation 21, with the exception of one part that is *assumed* and not stated—that the Holy City is a cube or foursquare in form. It is possible, however, that the New Jerusalem is in the form of a *pyramid* and not a *cube*.

The most recognized pyramid shape is that of the large stone pyramids in Egypt, some constructed over 4,500 years ago. The creation of Adam dates back on our known chronology to about 6,000 years; thus the concept of the pyramid shape could have been known or used sometime prior to the flood of Noah, which occurred about 1,658 years from Adam.

These pyramids were large, triangular-shaped tombs made of rock that housed the mummified bodies of Egyptian pharaohs, their family members, and their wealth. The pyramids have a four-sided square base with rows of steps that form a four-sided triangle that narrows to a point at the top.

There is a lot of tradition and speculation about where the pyramid *shape* originated and who actually supervised the building of the Egyptian pyramids. With the enormous size of many pyramid stones, it is possible that the race of giants who once lived on the earth were involved in the physical building process. As previously mentioned, these giants still would have been on the earth, especially the Middle East, at the time of the pyramid construction.

Various early church fathers pointed out that these fallen angels and giants were the basis for the corrupt mythology among the Greek poets and philosophers. This theory of giants being the offspring of fallen angels was believed in the time of Christ, and was only changed in the fourth century by Julias Africanus (see: *The Wilmington's Guide to the Bible*–Fallen Angels and Giants–Page 25).

It is also interesting to note that among the ancient Sumerians—a people group who lived in ancient Mesopotamia—these "star gods" were to be worshipped on mountain peaks, and if they did not have them, they built them. (This correlates to Satan and his angels having once worshipped on the Holy Mountain in heaven). Thus the ancient people were fully aware of these demi-gods, and wrote about them in ancient records.

Angels can also appear as *strangers unaware*, meaning they can manifest as a person and those around them will be unaware they are angels (Heb. 13:2). The angels, who before and after the flood participated in demi-god procreation, were at some point removed from earth, being labeled fallen angels that are now bound in tartarus (hell) under the earth (2 Pet. 2:4). These angels had been in heaven, in the heavenly temple of God, and also saw the construction of the New Jerusalem, in ages past, which brings us back to the original thought: the shape of the New Jerusalem.

NOT NECESSARILY A CUBE

From the time I was a child, every minister I heard described the New Jerusalem as the "foursquare city," or the "cube-shaped Holy City." However, read carefully John's description:

> "The city is laid out as a square; its length is as great as its breadth. And he measured the city with the reed: twelve thousand

furlongs. Its length, breadth, and height are equal. Then he measured its wall: one hundred and forty-four cubits, according to the measure of a man, that is, of an angel."

– REVELATION 21:16-17

Nowhere in John's description is the city described as cubical, or a fifteen-hundred-mile-square shape. John wrote that the city's foundation is laid out in an equal square pattern of twelve thousand furlongs, which translates to about fifteen hundred miles square, with the foundation laid out north to south and east to west. The length and width are equal to the height; meaning that from the base to top is also twelve thousand furlongs, or fifteen hundred miles high. It has been *assumed* that the city is cubical in shape.

However, the New Jerusalem could also be pyramid-shaped, since a pyramid has a square base with four equal sides rising to a narrow point at the top. There are four directions—north, south, east and west—and the four-square pyramid base is the shape of the four-square brass altar and golden altar, both with four horns on the four corners that represent the four directions of the earth.

THE GREAT PYRAMID IN GIZA

One of the seven manmade wonders of the ancient world is the Great Pyramid in Giza, Egypt. Constructed about 4,500 years ago, it took just under thirty years to complete. It is noted that the corners of the base of the pyramid align with the four points of a compass—north, south, east and west. The Pyramid has about 2,300,000 limestone blocks that weigh 2.5 to 30 tons, with a few weighing 50 tons. According to the historian Herodotus, who visited Egypt about 450 B.C., the pyramid would have required over 100,000 people working three months out of the year to complete the structure. With the massive stones and height, even Egyptologists and archeologists are uncertain how it was built.

This pyramid is 90,000,000 cubic feet. With its stones, you could build thirty empire state buildings, and it is as high as a modern, forty-eight story building. It includes three burial chambers; the first is carved in bedrock. The second was identified by early explorers as the queen's chamber and is located above the burial chamber. The third, the king's chamber, was situated almost directly in the center of the pyramid and is accessed by walking through a twenty-six-foot-high grand gallery.

Why would a pharaoh spend many years having tens of thousands of workers build a death monument for him? Remember that the pharaohs were not just royal kings; Egyptians also considered them gods. They believed in an afterlife in which the soul would migrate to another realm. The pharaohs' bodies and their wealth were encased in the inner chambers of the pyramids, because the Egyptians believed this would allow the pharaoh to transfer his wealth into the next life.

Researchers note that, in the earlier days, the outer pyramid had 144,000 polished casting stones covering it. This number is Biblically significant, as 144,000 Jewish men will appear on the heavenly mount Zion in Revelation 14:1-5.

When the sun hit these polished stones, the pyramid shone like a jewel. It has been suggested that the white stones acted like a mirror or a shining star, and the reflection from the sun hitting the stones was so powerful that the pyramid could have been seen from the moon. Among the ancient Egyptians, the pyramid was called *ikhet*, meaning the glorious light.

Oddly, for no known reason, the capstone is missing from the top of the great pyramid. However, in the beginning, Satan was a bearer of light, a morning star, when the heavenly Jerusalem first was being created. Just as the great pyramid is missing its capstone, I believe this correlates to Satan falling from heaven before the upper section of the New Jerusalem was completed.

The pyramid is aligned *true north* (with only 3/60th of degree error). Biblically, the *northern* part of heaven is the most important, as the planet heaven is located in another galaxy, in the northern region of the cosmos (Isa. 14:13; Ps. 48:2; Ezek. 1:4). The descending chamber in the pyramid was aligned to the North Star in the day it was created. The pyramid is built in the center of the land masses, where the east-west-north-south axes cross. One of the greatest unexplained great pyramid mysteries is the type of mortar that was used, which is stronger than stone and still holds up today. The composition has undergone testing, but to this day has never been reproduced.

From the creation of Adam to the present age is estimated to be close to 6,000 years. If the pyramid was built 4,500 years ago and the flood of Noah was 1,658 years from Adam, then the pyramid was constructed before the flood. In fact, it might have been constructed about the same time Noah was building the ark. This timeframe runs parallel to the time when the fallen angels were impregnating the daughters of men and producing the giants (Gen 6:1-4).

Could giants have helped moved these massive stones, and could the shape and the mysterious cosmic alignments in the pyramid have been revealed by a fallen angel, who had expert knowledge of cosmic bodies and creation mysteries? Angels would have had astonishing insight into the cosmic mysteries, long before modern telescopes and NASA space travel.

Another interesting aspect is the controversy concerning the meaning of the word *pyramid*. It comes from the Greek words *pyramis* and *pyramidos*. Some suggest the mysterious meaning of pyramis may refer to the shape of the pyramid. However, American Egyptologist Mark Lehner researched the ancient meaning of words for pyramid and translated them as "the place of ascension," referring to the chamber in the pyramid where the soul of the dead pharaoh ascended to the afterlife.

Some researchers have been fascinated at the energy levels found inside the pyramids chambers, and believe the pyramid shape is a type of energy capacitor. Some suggest the meaning of the word pyramid (pyramidos), based on their own translation of the word from various sources, means, "fire in the middle," and refers to the king's chamber.

It would have taken a special revelation for the Egyptians or someone among them to discover the significance of the pyramid shape and align it so precisely in the building process. However, if we consider that these were angels in human embodiment, they would have known the contours of the New Jerusalem, and been in heaven while it was being constructed. Since these angels lived on earth among men until they were removed and confined in the underworld (2 Pete 2:4), it is possible that the pyramid formation was designed as a *miniature replica of the heavenly Jerusalem.*

I suggest that the fallen angels that roamed the earth prior to the flood would have known the shape of the Holy City in heaven, and may have attempted to replicate it through the shapes of the numerous pyramids built not only in Egypt, but throughout the world. It was believed that a capstone was prepared for the top, but was rejected by the builders. This in interesting in light of a prophecy concerning Christ:

> "The stone which the builders rejected has become the chief cornerstone."
>
> – PSALMS 118:22

> "Jesus said to them, 'Have you never read in the Scriptures: The stone which the builders rejected has become the chief cornerstone. This was the Lord's doing, and it is marvelous in our eyes'?"
>
> – MATTHEW 21:42

Lucifer, the original light bearer in heaven, never completed the building project on the pyramid city, the New Jerusalem, as he was expelled from the stones of fire before the upper stones were set in place in the walls. On the earthly great pyramid, the top stones are missing. However, Christ, the rejected stone, has become chief cornerstone of the kingdom! The fallen morning star has been replaced by Christ, the Morning Star who will one day light the entire city of New Jerusalem from within. Neither the sun nor moon will be required for light, as the glory of God and the Christ is the radiance and light of the city (Rev. 21:23).

THE LOCATION OF THE CITY

If you take a map of the United States and place a 1,500 square-mile foundation of the New Jerusalem over America, it would stretch from the coast of Virginia to the middle of the state of Colorado, and from the bottom tip of Florida to the top of Maine. When the city descends to earth after the purification of the earth by fire, assuming the land mass on earth remains the same, which continent would the city rest on for all eternity? Since it is the New Jerusalem, it will replace the earthly Jerusalem; but the current city of Jerusalem and the nation of Israel itself are too small for such a massive city.

However, when God made His covenant with Abraham and promised the patriarch a land grant everywhere the soles of his feet would touch, God then gave the precise location of the land Abraham's descendants would inherit:

> "On the same day the Lord made a covenant with Abram, saying: "To your descendants I have given this land, from the river of Egypt to the great river, the River Euphrates."
>
> – GENESIS 15:18

In the time of David and Solomon, the kingdom of Israel had expanded south to the river Sichor (called the River of Egypt). This river bordered modern-day Egypt and Israel, then flowed northward into Lebanon and Syria, and extended to Damascus (2 Sam. 8:3; 2 Chron. 9:26). The promise of the future Jewish land grant also extends into the tribal region of parts of Arabia. From the River of Egypt to the Euphrates, and from Israel's Mediterranean coast, into Israel, Jordan and northern Arabia is about 1,500 square miles. The New Jerusalem could easily descend onto earth in the land called the Middle East, within the same boundaries promised to Abraham over 4,000 years ago!

When the moment arrives *for heaven to come down on earth,* the landscape will be completely altered from its present condition. Just as Noah's flood changed the surface of the planet, the intense heat from the fiery renovation of earth will evaporate the oceans, as on the new earth there is "no more sea" (Rev. 21:1). The main water source will be the crystal clear River of Life flowing within the Holy City (Rev. 22:1-2).

Using the pyramid imagery, if we place God's throne in the position of the capstone, with the rays of glorious light shooting forth into all four corners of the base foundation, we can see how the entire city would be lit with the light of the Lamb of God. Imagine a clear river that may begin 1,500 miles high within the city, and cascade downward into the foundation of the city. Certainly we have never imagined the stunning beauty and possibilities of things to come.

When the New Jerusalem descends to earth, the Holy City will be the eternal home of the saints of all ages, the holy angels, and Christ. From the fall of Adam until the crucifixion of Christ, the spirits of righteous men were taken into the underworld into a massive chamber called Abraham's Bosom (Luke 16). When Christ was raised from the dead, He led those captives into freedom and brought those souls into paradise in the third heaven, because His death and resurrection prepared us a place in heaven. Also, living men required an earthly High Priest to make intercession for their sins. Christ, however, opened up direct access to God, and will one day take us from earth to His heavenly dwelling.

CHAPTER 9

Spirits of the Righteous Made Perfect

GOD LOVES MOUNTAINS. The original creation of the heavens began on a designated holy mountain in the celestial third heaven. Much later, Abraham was instructed to give up Isaac on one of the mountains in the land of Moriah (Gen. 22:1-3). Fourteen generations passed when David pitched his worship tent upon Mount Zion (1 Chron. 15-16), and Solomon built the sacred Temple of God on Mount Moriah (2 Chron. 3).

Elijah challenged the false prophets of Baal on the top of Mount Carmel (I Kings 18). Christ was transfigured in the presence of Elijah and Moses on a high mountain (Matt. 17:1-3). Christ arose early before sunrise to pray on a high mountain, one of many rocky crests that tower above and surround the Sea of Galilee (Matt. 14:23). Christ sealed mankind's redemption from a hill called Golgotha (Matt. 27:33). The tribe of Judah received a tribal land grant that has some of the most beautiful, rust and rose colored mountains of any other tribe in Israel.

The heathen were mystified by the height and beauty of Israel's rugged mountains, which they demonstrated when they built their groves to numerous idols and false gods on Israel's highest mountain ranges. When Israel repossessed Abraham's Promised Land and expelled the heathen tribes, one of their main assignments was to search the tops of the mountains, tear down the tribal altars, destroy pagan groves, and break the clay and stone idols, as the true God must always sit higher than man's false images (Exod. 34:13; Deut. 7:5).

When the dead in Christ arise and the living are changed and caught up, the family of God will unite on a mountain in heaven called Mount Zion. The apostle Paul caught a glimpse of the spirits of the righteous gathered with the angels on this sacred heavenly mountain:

> "But you have come to Mount Zion and to the city of the living God, the heavenly Jerusalem, to an innumerable company of angels, to the general assembly and church of the firstborn who are registered in heaven, to God the Judge of all, to the spirits of just men made perfect."
>
> – HEBREWS 12:22-23

The word "just" is an old English word used in the 1611 translation to describe a person who is righteous before God, and holy and pure in their moral character. The *righteous* and not the *religious* will inherit the heavenly city. The majority of world religions believe in some type of heaven, paradise or afterlife, although each group has its own teaching on how its followers gain access to this mysterious realm. Religion will give you access to a religious temple or mosque, but heaven is a city with its own registry—the Lamb's book of life (Rev. 21:27)—and is accessed only through a *covenant relationship* with God.

Many who penned the parchments we call the Scriptures were prophets and apostles whose eyes pierced the natural veil to see into the celestial world of God, angels, and the spirits of just men. Their accounts are written throughout the pages of the Holy Word of God.

Heaven is the proper name for the vast, cosmic expanse that stretches above and beyond the clouds, and extends for millions of light years in all directions. The solar heavens house nine recognized planets: Mercury, Venus, Earth, Mars, Saturn, Jupiter, Neptune, Uranus, and Pluto (although recently some have omitted Pluto), plus trillions of stars, nebulas, colorful pockets of gases, and cosmic dust splattered like bright, colorful paint purposefully slung on an artist's canvas.

Physicists who study the cosmic heavens—many of whom make no claim to Christianity or any other religion—say that one word sums up the entire cosmos: *energy*. They say the universe is continually expanding with something called "dark energy." One physicist speculates that, in thirty billion years, the entire universe will expand until the pull of gravity is lost and everything eventually falls apart. Others suggests that in the same timeframe, within millions of years, the strong gravity from within a mysterious black hole will suck the entire galaxy into it, eventually leaving nothing but dark space.

Somewhere, millions of light years away on the edge of space as we know it, in the northern section of the cosmos is a place known as the third heaven (2 Cor. 12:2)—the name given for the general dwelling place of God. It is a specific place in the highest, outer heaven; it is God's dwelling place from ages past and ages to come (Rev. 1:8).

What image comes to your mind when you hear a message on the subject of heaven? In my childhood I imagined a massive platform suspended in space, similar to the famous Star Trek movies. I thought it was a huge, crystal floor floating on nothing.

It appears from Scriptural evidence that heaven is a *planet*, similar to earth. The size compared to the earth is uncertain, as the earth is 25,000 miles in circumference at the equator, and the planet heaven could be much larger. Others suggest, since the earth has so many patterns of heaven concealed in the Tabernacle, the Temple, Jerusalem, and the creation narrative, that the planet heaven could be the same size as earth.

God's eternal dwelling has three distinct and significant sections. The first is the *Temple of God*. This is the sacred mountain of God in heaven (the heavenly Mount Zion—Rev. 14:1) that the prophets often described in their visions. Ezekiel described God on a sapphire throne in Ezekiel 1:26. Isaiah observed the Lord sitting high on His throne with a flowing *robe* (a 'train' in the KJV) filling the heavenly temple (Isa. 6:1). In the Apocalypse, the Apostle John gave a remarkable firsthand description of God's eternal, royal throne room, including the sacred worship, the crystal floor, the throne itself, and the heavenly living creatures in continual worship.

This region of heaven will be where many activities take place, such as worship, the release of angelic judgment on earth, and the Judgment

Seat of Christ called the Bema (Rev. 11:18), which occurs while the future tribulation is unleashed on earth. The original heavenly furniture that Moses saw—furniture that provided the pattern for the holy furniture in the wilderness Tabernacle—is found in this eternal temple: the Menorah (Rev. 1:12), the Golden Altar (Rev. 8:3-4), and the Ark of the Covenant (Rev. 11:19).

The second distinct section of heaven is the famous holy city, the *New Jerusalem*, which was described by John in Revelation 21. Even Abraham, the first Hebrew patriarch, looked for this city, as we read, "For he looked for a city which hath foundations, whose builder and maker is God" (Heb.11:10). The city was constructed in a large section of heaven in eternity past, and after the thousand year reign of Christ, the fifteen-hundred-square-mile city will come down from God out of heaven to a new earth (Rev. 21:1-3). The New Jerusalem will be the most elaborate and expensive housing complex in the universe!

The third region is identified as *paradise*, and it serves as the temporary abode of the departed souls and spirits of the *righteous* people who once lived on earth but have died. Paradise is a resting place for those who die *in Christ*, from the time of Christ's redemptive ministry to the resurrection of the dead in Christ, which occurs at the coming of the Lord (1 Thess. 4:16-17). This large paradise area is located somewhere in the third heaven (2 Cor. 12:2-4).

One possible clue to the location of paradise is found in Revelation 6:9-11:

> *"And when he had opened the fifth seal, I saw under the altar the souls of them that were slain for the word of God, and for the testimony which they held: And they cried with a loud voice, saying, How long, O Lord, holy and true, dost thou not judge and avenge our blood on them that dwell on the earth?*

> *"And white robes were given unto every one of them; and it was said unto them, that they should rest yet for a little season, until their fellow servants also and their brethren, that should be killed as they were, should be fulfilled."*

In the setting of this narrative, John is in heaven standing before the throne of God on a floor that appears to be as large as a sea, yet it looks like crystal. Sitting on the floor before God's throne is a golden altar (Rev. 8:3). As John peered through the crystal floor, under the heavenly altar, he observed a countless multitude dressed in white robes. These are the souls and spirits of Christian martyrs, who are commanded to rest until others who will also be martyred for their testimony arrive (Rev. 6:11).

This imagery has all of the important elements to identify paradise as being situated *underneath* this massive crystal floor. This would mean that, if the martyrs looked up through the crystal, they would see a flowing prism of colors radiating the glory of God from above, where God is sitting on His throne.

Do Spirits Linger Three Days?

One of the questions I have been asked is: When a believer dies, does the person's soul and spirit linger outside the body for a period of time, or does it make its way immediately to its eternal dwelling?

In the story of the raising of Lazarus, Christ was informed that His friend was sick, yet He remained in the city where He was ministering. He eventually arrived at Bethany on the *fourth day* after Lazarus was dead (John 11:17). In those days, commoners were not embalmed at death, but were wrapped in linen and placed in a cave-like tomb with a large stone covering the opening.

Why would Christ wait until the fourth day to raise His friend? There are several possible reasons. First, Jesus knew by the Holy Spirit that Lazarus had died, as He had said, "He sleepeth and I go that I might awake him..." (John 11:11). The word *sleep* has more than one meaning, and sometimes is used in the New Testament as a metaphor for someone who *died*.

The Greek word for a person who is physically or spiritually asleep is *katheudo*, meaning to lie down and rest or to literally fall asleep. It is used of the disciples falling asleep in the Garden of Gethsemane (Matt. 26:45; Mark 14:41; Luke 22:46). When Paul used the metaphor of a believer who had died, calling it *sleep*, the word is *koimao*, which means to slumber, but figuratively means to be deceased (1 Cor. 11:30; 15:51; 1 Thess. 4:14). It is interesting that, in the story of Lazarus, the word "sleep" is found three different times, and all three times a different Greek word is used.

Jesus desired to "awaken Lazarus out of his sleep." This word *sleep* is *exegeiro*, and Jesus is saying He wants Lazarus to fully arise, to resuscitate, to release—in this case, to release from death. The disciples thought Christ was indicating Lazarus was sick and was simply taking a rest. We read, "Then His disciples said, 'Lord, if he sleeps, he will get well.' " This word sleep is *koimao*, meaning to put to sleep, and figuratively can refer to death. "Howbeit Jesus spake of His death: but they thought that He had spoken of taking a rest in sleep" (John 11:13). This word sleep is *hupnos*, and refers to a stupor in which a person becomes drowsy and sleeps. To the disciples, Lazarus' sickness made him sleepy, and this was good. However, Christ knew he had died.

In Christ's day there was a tradition that, when a person died, their spirit departed from the body but remained near the burial tomb, hovering near the body. Once the spirit saw the body decaying—which happened by the fourth day, they believed the spirit was sent to its eternal abode. By Christ delaying His trip to Bethany, the spirit of Lazarus should already be at its eternal resting place and unable to make the journey back across the eternal divide and into a corrupt, stinking body.

In the Lazarus story, when Christ told His disciples that Lazarus was dead, Thomas spoke up and said, "Let us also go, that we may die with Him." (John 11:16). Was Thomas depressed or despondent to want to go to Bethany and die with Lazarus? In the previous chapter, we see that Christ was in Jerusalem and the people attempted to stone Him for a controversial message He preached, but Christ escaped out of their hands (see John 10:33-39). Throughout the Scripture, when men became discouraged, some wanted to die. Both Elijah and Moses became so despondent that they asked God to let them die (Exod. 32:33; 1 Kings 19:4). Thomas suggested that all of the disciples die with Christ at Bethany. Even Paul was willing to die while attending a feast in Jerusalem (Acts 21:13).

LINGER OR GO?

Does our spirit linger or does it take flight? The clear evidence from Scripture indicates that angels carry the departed spirit immediately to its eternal destination, which is the heavenly paradise if the deceased is a believer. When the poor, hungry beggar died near a rich man's door as dogs licked his sores, the rich man also died and immediately opened his eyes in hell. The beggar, however, was carried by the angels to a secure and peaceful chamber identified as Abraham's bosom (see Luke 16:19-23).

At the moment of Christ's death, He cried out, "It is finished," and He "gave up the ghost," indicating that His spirit was released from His body. Paul revealed that Christ (His spirit) descended into the lower parts of the earth (the underworld) and preached to the spirits in prison (Eph. 4:8-9; 1 Pet. 3:18-19) during the three days His body was encased in the tomb. The body ceased all activity, yet the spirit continued its activity outside of the body.

There have been many believers who died in an accident, or during a massive heart attack, or some form of sudden, near death experience who describe themselves being separated from their bodies and seeing the mangled metal of an automobile, or hearing the doctors say, "We have lost him." They describe having a heightened use of all five senses, and their physical sight seems to expand to 360 degrees as their hearing becomes highly sensitive to all the sounds around them.

Imagine if the person who was taken through death by the horrific accident lingered for three days as some ancients believed, and could see their body being hauled to the morgue, watch the family cry in grief, and observe the entire death preparation process. For a believer who left their body and headed to heaven, this three-day observation period could be a troubling and difficult sight. The grieving process is for the living and not to be observed by the departed.

The instant process of the spirit and soul's departure can be illustrated when the Apostle John saw a vision of Christ and received a message to the seven churches. After completing his admonition and warnings, we read, "And after this a door was opened in heaven...and immediately I was in the Spirit and beheld a throne in heaven..." (Rev. 4:1-2). John was physically on a desolate, rocky island in the middle of the Aegean Sea; yet in a moment's flash, he was suddenly in the throne room. When people close their eyes in death, they immediately open them in the next world.

The first martyr in the book of Acts was a deacon named Stephen. This man of faith preached a detailed message to a Jewish audience and quoted Jewish history and Old Testament narratives to emphasize that Christ is the Messiah. This conclusion disturbed the devout, law-abiding Jewish crowd, especially when Stephen saw a vision and cried out, "Behold, I see the heavens opened, and the Son of man standing on the right hand of God" (Acts 7:56). They closed their ears and dragged him out of the city, where they stoned him to death. As the rocks were pelting his flesh, as his bones were breaking and blood flowed down his face, we read, "And they stoned Stephen, (as he was) calling upon God, and saying, 'Lord Jesus, receive my spirit' " (Acts 7:59). The reason Stephen saw Christ standing, I believe, is the Lord was preparing to receive Stephen's spirit immediately in heaven, the moment his life ceased.

THE SPIRIT AWAITS THE RESURRECTION

After Christ's resurrection, the righteous souls who were located in the underworld were moved to the third heaven. Imagine standing at the death bed of a righteous believer, who is preparing to be transferred from earth to heaven, as angels separate the soul and spirit from the human body and escort the believer directly into heaven.

Time is far different in heaven than on earth. The Scripture reveals that a day with the Lord is as a thousand years and a thousand years as one day (Psalms 90:4). Because time is far different in the eternal realm, I believe that the departed souls who have been in heaven for hundreds of years based on earth time, are unaware of the actual time they have been in paradise. As the Scripture states, if a thousand years are as one day (2 Pet. 3:8), then the early church saints who passed

1900 years ago may feel as though they have been in heaven but a couple of days!

The book of Revelation speaks of *days and nights*. Notice that the living creatures worshipping God around God's throne have "no rest day or night, saying Holy, Holy, Holy, Lord God Almighty..." (Rev. 4:8). There is a holy remnant that will serve God day and night in His temple (Rev. 7:15). Satan is the accuser of the brethren before God day and night (Rev. 12:10). The idea of night in heaven seems odd, and we read that in the New Jerusalem, there is no night there (Rev. 21:25; 22:5). The phrase "day and night" is used for human comprehension and not to define an eternal God abiding in a time zone. He is the beginning and the end of all things and He never ages.

Because God's supernal glory radiates from His face and His throne throughout heaven, the atmosphere is absolute light in all directions. It seems odd that heaven would experience night, as night is a daily cycle that enables men to rest, then arise at sunrise to work. In heaven our *labors cease* and our rest is not in the form of sleep, but rest from our physical work and spiritual struggles. The phrases in Revelation concerning day and night may refer to a continual, non-stop frame of activity. God never sleeps nor slumbers (Psa. 121:4), Christ continually makes intercession, and the angels of God require no sleep. It is difficult to imagine having the ability to stay alert and awake continually, never needing physical rest. But outside of the human body, time restraints are removed and the eternal spirit lives in eternal, endless motion.

The departed spirits of men, women, and children await the first resurrection of the dead in Christ, which will occur at Christ's return to gather the believers together unto Him. Paul wrote that when Christ descends from heaven with a shout, the voice of the archangel, and the trumpet of God, He will bring the spirits of the departed with Him:

> "For if we believe that Jesus died and rose again, even so God will bring with Him those who sleep in Jesus."
>
> – 1 Thessalonians 4:14 (NKJV)

The reason for bringing those who sleep (the departed) with Him is to raise their bodies and join them with their spirits, thus creating a new, resurrected body—the same type of body that Christ received when He rose from the dead. The new body can travel from place to place by thought, and can move through solid objects such as a closed door. (John 20:19, 26). The resurrected body has a tangible feel and can be held, touched, and seen—all of which occurred after Christ's resurrection (John 20:27-29).

At this present time, the bodies of departed saints are buried on the earth, but their souls and spirits are already in the presence of the Lord. They are not yet "perfected," but are in a realm of total awareness and activity. Christ predicted His resurrection from the dead when He said to His followers, "Go, tell that fox (Herod), Behold, I cast out demons and perform cures today and tomorrow, and the third day I shall be perfected" (Luke 13:32-33). Christ was sinless, pure, and totally righteous, yet was not "perfected" until He was raised from the dead. This perfection included a resurrected body that was in perfect health and could never die again or suffer in any manner. It included a body that was not limited by physical restraints. His body was no longer limited by locations and distances, as Christ could suddenly appear or disappear with the blink of an eye or the speed of thought. *He was a spiritually perfect man in an imperfect body until His resurrection, when He became a perfect man in a perfect body!*

On earth, our souls and spirits are locked in a physical shell that is subject to earthly curses and crisis. When the resurrected saints, being changed into immortal beings, walk through the gates of heavenly Zion, they will be the spirits of just men and women made perfect (Heb. 12:23).

In Hebrews 12:23, the word "perfect" is the Greek word *teleioo*, and can mean to *consummate, complete, or accomplish an end to something.* How can our spirit be made perfect? Biblically, the human spirit is sensitive to negative emotions. Your human spirit can be heavy, grieved, sorrowful, overwhelmed, and sensitive to pain. Once we have received our resurrected and glorified bodies, our spirits will be perfected, completely whole and forever free from fear, anxiety, burdens, pain, and sorrow. This is emphasized in Revelation 21:4, where John wrote, "And God will wipe away every tear from their eyes; there shall be no more death, nor sorrow, nor crying. There shall be no more pain, for the former things have passed away."

In the beginning of time, the anointed Cherub was created perfect until "iniquity was found in him" (Ezek. 28:15). At the end of time, those among humanity *born in iniquity* (Psa. 51:5) and who received Christ's redemptive covenant will be made perfect, as no iniquity will be found in them!

CHAPTER 10

Pre-Born Infants in Heaven

OR CENTURIES THERE has been theological debate about infants in paradise. Most acknowledge, once an infant enters the world through the birth process and breathes on its own, that if the child were to pass away, its soul and spirit would be taken into the heavenly paradise. This is borne out when Bathsheba was pregnant with David's son. The child was born with a terrible affliction, which led David to engage in a seven-day vigil of prayer and fasting. On the seventh day the infant died. Under Divine inspiration, David said, *"But now he is dead, wherefore should I fast? Can I bring him back again? I shall go to him, but he shall not return to me"* (2 Samuel 12:23).

What did David mean, "I will go to him?" The early Biblical patriarchs understood that at death, the soul and spirit leave the body and are taken to a special place to await the resurrection of the dead. In the 1611 King James translation, this process is called "giving up the ghost," or we might say "releasing the spirit from the body."

This death process is alluded to with Abraham (Gen 25:8), Ishmael (Gen. 25:17), Isaac (35:29), and Jacob (Gen. 49:33). Once their spirits departed their bodies, each spirit was "gathered to his people." Some suggest this means they were buried in the same place. However, the phrase refers to the gathering chamber once concealed under the earth, in which righteous souls in covenant with God were gathered together. At the resurrection of Christ, those righteous souls were transported to the third heaven, where today they wait in paradise.

Thus David knew that once the eternal spirit of his infant son departed to its final resting place, he could not bring him back; but one day, he would go to where he was—meaning that when David died, he would see his son again.

What about an infant who dies inside the womb? When does the eternal soul and spirit enter the physical body of an infant? After years of researching this, it seems there are three possible theories:

1. The soul and spirit enter the womb at the moment of conception;

2. The soul and spirit enter the womb when the infant is six months old;

3. The soul and spirit enter the infant after the umbilical cord is cut.

Ministers and theologians have varying opinions and either accept or reject each theory. The first point to ponder is the foreknowledge of God in the human conception process. In the eyes of God, the unborn is a living soul and not just a blob of tissue, or even a creature with muscle, skin and bone.

In Genesis 25:21-22, Rebekah, the wife of Isaac, was pregnant with twins. As the two twins were developing inside the womb, we read that "the children struggled within her" (Gen 25:22). Notice the inspired Word of God called them *children* prior to their actual birth.

In Luke 1:39-44, Mary informed Elizabeth that she had been visited by an angel and was impregnated to carry the Messiah. Elizabeth called Mary "the mother of my Lord," before Christ was ever born in Bethlehem. Mary is called a mother, a title given to someone who has a child.

Elizabeth and her husband had prayed for many years to conceive a child. The Lord opened her womb and gave her a son named John. Elizabeth was six months pregnant with John when Mary announced her own pregnancy. In Luke 1:41-44, Elizabeth felt John move in her belly and said to Mary, "The babe leaped in my womb."

The Greek word *babe* here is *brephos* and is used four times by Luke, referring to John the Baptist and Christ. The interesting point is that the same word is used by Luke (who was a medical doctor) when the infant is still *in* the womb and once the infant is *outside* the womb. The word *brephos* can refer to an unborn child (Luke 1:41), a newborn child, or an older infant (Luke 2:12; 18:15; Acts 7:19; 2 Tim. 3:15). If it is *not a baby* in your womb, then you are not pregnant. The fact is that a child is a child and a living being *in the womb*, as well as outside the womb.

Notice that Elizabeth said that John "leaped for joy" (Luke 1:44). The angel Gabriel had informed John's father, Zacharias, that John would be "filled with the Holy Ghost, even from his mother's womb" (Luke 1:15). The Holy Spirit enters the human spirit and resides there. For John to be filled from his mother's womb would require John to have an eternal spirit within his small body while he was in the womb of his mother. The infilling of John appears to have occurred when he was six months of age, as this was the same time he leaped in his mother's womb, and his mother, Elizabeth, was instantly filled with the Holy Spirit (Luke 1:41). Perhaps when the Spirit filled John, his own mother received her infilling within her innermost being!

WHY ARE CHILDREN CALLED "SEED?"

God Himself identifies children with the word "seed." In the Old Testament, God addressed future fathers, such as Abraham, by calling his unborn children "seed" (NKJ - Gen. 12:7; 22:17). God uses the term seed because children begin in the loins of their fathers, as it requires the seed of a man to create the infant in the mother's womb. Contemporary men call this "seed" sperm, but the Bible called it seed for a good reason.

Just as an apple seed planted in the earth has all the characteristics of a future apple tree—the roots, trunk, branches, leaves, and fruit—concealed in the seed, so the physical features of a child are encoded in the DNA of the father's seed. Eve was the first on record to use the word seed after Seth's birth, as she said, "God hath appointed me another seed instead of Abel, whom Cain slew" (Gen. 4:25). Eve may have used this word seed, since God Himself had stated that the "seed of the woman" would bruise the head of the serpent (Gen. 3:15).

With Abraham came the "mark of the covenant," which was circumcision of the foreskin on the Jewish male child eight days after his birth (Gen. 17:12). Each male child shed blood during circumcision. Once he married and consummated with his wife, the seed from his loins passed through the mark of circumcision, thus marking his seed for a future blessing from God.

Paul confirmed this when he wrote about Abraham paying tithe (in Jerusalem) to Melchizedek, the first king and priest:

> "Even Levi, who receives tithes, paid tithes through Abraham, so to speak, for he was still in the loins of his father when Melchizedek met him."

> – HEBREW 7:9-10

CONCEPTION AND BIRTH ARE MARKED

Since God Himself is the giver of life and the creator, He alone should be the voice of inspiration to explain to the medical field when life begins. In Scripture the moment of conception is marked as the moment life begins. Genesis 25:21-22, 2 Kings 19:3 and Ruth 1:11 all speak of children and sons in the womb. Job 3:3 speaks of both birth and conception. In Luke 1:36 we read where Elizabeth conceived a son, and in Luke 1:57 she brought forth (gave birth to) a son. The infant was a son at conception, and nine months later a son at birth.

God alone has the attribute of foreknowledge, meaning that He has detailed information on each person before they are conceived. Nine months before their son was born, Abraham and Sarah were told his name would be called Isaac (Gen. 17:19). Nine months before Samson's birth, his father Menoah was informed he would have a son, and he would be a Nazarite. Before John was conceived in his mother's womb, the angel told his father that he would be a son, he would be called John, he would come in the spirit of Elijah, and be filled with the Spirit from his mother's womb (Luke 1:13). The angel Gabriel brought Mary a message that she would conceive a son whose name would be Jesus, and He would save his people from their sins (Matt. 1:21). Note that in three of the four examples—Isaac, John, and Jesus—the name of the son was given before conception.

Throughout Scripture we find times when God revealed the gender of children before their birth; at times, He revealed their names, destinies, purposes, and plans for their future. God especially marked kings, prophets, and priests, as their ministry would impact the nation of Israel.

Hundreds of years before their births, the Holy Spirit revealed the names of two important leaders, Josiah (1 Kings 13:2) and Cyrus (Isa. 44:28). The destinies of these two men would directly affect Israel and the Jewish people.

THE SPIRIT WITHIN INFANTS

In Ecclesiastes 11:5.Solomon wrote:

> "As you know not what is the way of the spirit, nor how the bones do grow in the womb of her that is with child: even so you know not the works of God who makes all."

Notice how the spirit and the bones are growing in the womb. A prime example is with Christ. In the miracle of the incarnation, Christ, who pre-existed with God, left his position in heaven to enter the womb of a virgin. For nine months, His body grew within Mary until the fullness of time, when He arrived in Bethlehem. Hebrews 10:5 reads, "A body thou hast prepared me...."

Paul penned an interesting observation when he said:

> "For I was alive without the law once; but when the commandment came, sin revived and I died."
>
> > - ROMANS 7:9

The time Paul was "alive without the law" was when he was a child, innocent with no awareness of sin. We would call this *before the age of accountability*. This age varies among children and youth, as each individual has a different level of comprehension and understanding. Moving from childhood into maturity, Paul reached a level of understanding of the law, and the consequences of breaking the law. The conscience is the inner voice of the soul that rebukes or condemns a person when they knowingly sin or break the law. A child whose mind is simple, whose heart is sincere, and whose spirit is undefiled by the flesh is innocent until their understanding perceives—not just parental rules of right and wrong—but the law itself.

Christ understood this when He ministered and parents brought their children to be blessed by Him. While there are only a few examples in New Testament, Christ did say that the kingdom of heaven is made up of children (Matt. 19:14). Christ informed His adult audience that unless they be converted and become like children, they cannot enter the kingdom" (Matt. 18:3).

WHAT ABOUT A MISCARRIAGE?

While the Scripture does not use the word miscarriage, it does speak of an *untimely birth* in Job 3:16 (KJV). The correct rendering of this phrase is *stillborn*. Countless mothers have been devastated when their child was stillborn in the womb. When Job lost his wealth, his ten children and his health, he began to curse the day he was born (Job 3:1). We read in Job 3:16-19 (NKJV):

> "Or why was I not hidden like a stillborn child, like infants who never saw light? There the wicked cease from troubling, and there the weary are at rest. There the prisoners rest together; they do not hear the voice of the oppressor. The small and great are there, and the servant is free from his master."

Job knew that when an infant passes, that child will see no wickedness and be at rest. The "rest" refers to the soul and spirit remaining in a compartment (in Job's day it was under the earth) where the person ceases from their labor. The word "prisoners" means the captives, or the souls and spirits in the Old Testament who were captives under the earth.

Jesus ministered to these souls for three days when He was in the heart of the earth; and at His resurrection, He led captivity captive and gave gifts unto men (Eph. 4:8-10). Notice both the "small and great" are there. The word small in Hebrew is *qutan*, and refers to the least, the little, and figuratively, to small (or young) in age. This is the place where David's infant son went when he died seven days after his birth.

In another verse, Job speaks of what occurs within the womb when an infant dies:

> "Why died I not from the womb? why did I not give up the ghost when I came out of the belly?"
>
> – JOB 3:11

The same question is posed to the Almighty by Job, as he wishes he had passed before being born:

> "Wherefore then hast thou brought me forth out of the womb? Oh that I had given up the ghost, and no eye had seen me!"
>
> – JOB 10:18

Note in Job 3:11 that the infant has a spirit (KJV-ghost) in their small body in their mother's womb. The spirit can depart the body, either while still in the womb (stillborn), or shortly after the child leaves the womb (Job 10:18). With the eternal spirit dwelling in the infant while still encased in the mother's embryonic fluid, then this means the spirit is within the body while the body is within the womb. The spirit does not wait until the child leaves the womb and breathes on its own before it enters the body and brings life.

OUR PERSONAL EXPERIENCE

Pam and I were married for eight years before she became pregnant with our first child, a beautiful son named Jonathan Gabriel. In the late 1980s, prior to his conception, I experienced two separate dreams in which I saw two little girls. In the dream, one looked about five years old and the other was younger. The one child looked strong and in charge of the situation, but the younger almost seemed to have some type of bodily defect. I asked the older girl her name and she replied, "I am Amanda, the little girl you are going to have."

I immediately asked her about the other little girl and she replied, "This is my sister, Rochelle." I awoke and immediately woke up my wife to tell her what I dreamed. I told her that it appeared we would have two girls in the future. We had a book of baby names and looked up Amanda and Rochelle. Amazingly, Rochelle meant "from a little stone."

The dream was so convincing that I met with our partners in Pigeon Forge, Tennessee and told them I believed we would have a little girl. A few months later we discovered Pam was pregnant. We painted the room pink and bought dresses and girly things, but to our astonishment, a beautiful, blond-haired, blue-eyed boy was in her womb! We both were surprised but thrilled, especially since the Scripture taught that a male child that opens the womb (a firstborn son) was considered holy to the Lord.

Because of our intense travel schedule and the fact that we were seldom home, eleven years passed before we considered having more children. After returning from a long trip, I was lying on our bed when suddenly, on my left ankle, I felt the hand of a small child, as though it was trying to balance. I sat up and told Pam what just happened and immediately commented, "I believe this is a sign that we are to have another child!"

Pam became pregnant at age thirty-eight. We informed our family, friends, and ministry partners who knew about the dream eleven years earlier, and all were in agreement that the girls were coming. We wondered if they might be twins, although as I saw them, they appeared to be different ages.

Several weeks into the pregnancy, we were setting up all day Monday at the Grand Hotel Convention Center for our biggest meeting of the year. While eating at a restaurant across the road from the hotel, Pam felt pain and suddenly began to bleed. We headed back to the room, and were saddened to learn she miscarried the tiny baby that was growing in her.

After the miscarriage, Pam felt emotionally and physically as though she would be unable to carry another child. However, she did become pregnant again, and into the seventh month, the doctor placed her on bed rest. I told Pam this would be a girl. I had seen a healthy girl in my dream, and I advised Pam not to be fearful, but to rest and let others help around the house. On August 2, 2001, our precious girl arrived and we named her Amanda, based on the dream from about thirteen years earlier.

At our ages, we will not be having other children, except for spiritual children won to Christ through our ministry. The question we asked was, "What happened to Rochelle?" Should we have attempted to have children earlier, or was Rochelle the child that was miscarried? Several circumstances seem to indicate this is possible. When Pam began to ask the Lord why the infant was taken and never given a chance to live on earth, the Holy Spirit gave Pam a personal Word to comfort her. After hearing this word, I was reminded of the dreams in which Amanda was strong, but Rochelle appeared weak, as though she had some form of birth defect.

Many years later we received a sweet letter from a woman who did not know about Pam's miscarriage. The letter moved me to a river of tears mixed with joy. Leisia from Oak Hill, California penned her story.

Her only son, Levi, passed away and she had been in a season of great grief. She had consistently prayed to see him in heaven. One day she was lying on her bed and had an "out of the body experience" (note 2 Cor. 12:1-4), where she was taken into heaven. She saw her sister-in-law who had passed away seven months before her son. Leisia asked if she knew where Levi was and was told yes. She described being able to appear in one location in heaven and suddenly appear in another. She appeared at the location where her son was sitting in a large chair. He ran to her, grabbed her, and they hugged. She said that you don't have to talk, as you can read the other person's thoughts and feelings. Leisia noticed that Levi was growing a prickly beard, which was unusual because the medicine he took while living kept him from growing facial hair. She then wrote the following in her letter:

"This is not the reason for my letter today. The Lord moved on my heart to write you after another heavenly experience I had yesterday. I was praying before daybreak in the early hours of Friday, September 20, 2013. While I was praying, I either slipped off into a dream, or I had a vision and found myself in the waiting room of a grand assembly of God's people in heaven. I sat down next to a beautiful little girl.

She had a light complexion, beautiful eyes, a dainty nose, and the loveliest thick, black curly hair. She had the wisdom of the ancients, and when I sat next to her I knew she was Perry and Pam Stone's daughter. Nevertheless she was not Amanda. She smiled very big and as I sat down next to her she said, 'I know who you are. You are a godly woman...'

"The only thing I know is that somehow you both have a gorgeous little girl in heaven who is waiting for you! Please don't be offended at me, but it is true. I can't tell you how, but it is true. I've heard that sometimes women miscarry, but they don't realize it or maybe you are already aware of your little girl waiting in Glory..."

In my two dreams many years ago, Rochelle had dark hair. However, I also recalled she look weak in her eyes and not as strong as Amanda. In the back of my mind I can still remember what she looked like. In the dream, Rochelle was holding a small stuffed animal. The story reached another point in 2014 in Griffin, Georgia. I met a doctor who is also a very talented artist. She brought me a group of various drawings and paintings to view. When I saw one that she drew of a little girl holding a small stuffed animal, I almost went into shock. The drawing looked almost identical to Rochelle as I had seen her in the dream many years ago. I asked if I could purchase the drawing, as I wanted it in my office. I cried when I looked at it and still do occasionally.

ANOTHER AMAZING STORY

John Herston works with world missions. Years ago he experienced a stunning dream or vision in which he was with a young man in heaven, who appeared to be about thirteen years of age. This young man told his name and said, "I am the son of Dr. Cho." John knew that he referred to Paul Cho, who at that time pastored the world's largest church. Later, John was driving Dr. Cho around when he was impressed to bring up the dream / vision he had of Dr. Cho's son in heaven. Dr. Cho was amazed and told those in the car that, many years ago, his wife was pregnant and had a miscarriage. The name the boy had told John in heaven was the name Dr. Cho and his wife had chosen if they had a son!

Another unusual part of the story is that, from the moment John experienced the dream or vision, it would have been about thirteen years prior that Mrs. Cho miscarried. Since the miscarriage happened thirteen years ago and the young man appeared to be about thirteen, this may imply that, in some cases, the spirit of a miscarried child could grow to be a certain age, or grow to a level of maturity that matches the number of years they would have grown on earth.

Barton Green is a screenwriter and author, and a friend of mine and the ministry. Bart's grandfather was a noted minister named G.W. Lane, who passed away many years ago. G.W. never wore a three-piece suit, but was buried in one. Many years later, Bart began to experience heart problems and, on one occasion while in the hospital, he felt that he actually had died and his spirit departed from his body. During what he felt was an "out of the body experience," Bart found his soul (or spirit) walking in a thick fog toward a bright light. Eventually, he came to the silhouette of two men talking to one another.

As the fog lifted, he saw his grandfather, G.W. Lane, standing there in a three-piece suit similar to the one he was buried in. G.W. informed Bart that God was not finished with his work on earth, and he began to reveal several things he would complete. At the time, he was not working on those things, but later they began to manifest. After the conversation, G.W. began to walk away into the light. Barton attempted to follow G.W., but he turned and told Barton, "No. You cannot go with us." G.W., however, did say one more thing that stunned Barton. He said, "I should tell you…your son is proud of you."

As Barton sat across my desk at the VOE offices and related this story, he said, "At first that threw me off. This was a very real experience, but I never had a son. Then I remembered that, when I was married, my wife had a miscarriage. It is apparent that it was a son and today he is in heaven."

To me, the most mind-boggling part of this story is that his son was aware of who his father was and what he was doing on earth! How this is possible, remains a mystery.

When relating stories such as these, there are skeptics within the Christian community who use radio, television, and social media to criticize anyone who says they've had such an experience. One minister heard of a fellow minister who was caught up into heaven and saw friends who had passed, and he began to accuse this godly man of consulting the dead. In no story I have ever heard has anyone told me they were attempting to contact the "other side," or make contact with a departed loved one. In each story, it is a dream, vision, or near-death experience the individual is relaying. I also remind some followers of this negative, self-righteous minister that Moses—who had been dead for fifteen hundred years—appeared on the Mount of Transfiguration with Christ, and spoke with Him concerning His death in Jerusalem.

We must also remember that a person whom we say is dead has not actually ceased to exist. We see the physical shell of their body in a coffin, but we cannot see the ever-living soul and spirit which has made its journey to either paradise or hell. The fact is, the soul and spirit are more alert outside the body than when it resided within the body, as the body places the spirit under certain limitations.

When we look closely at the biblical Hebrew and Greek words that describe infants in the womb, it is obvious that a children is considered a living soul, both at conception and while growing inside the mother's womb. The child is just as much a living breathing infant in the womb as outside the womb. The soul and spirit originate with God, and they are implanted in the womb by God Himself.

Solomon wrote that, at death, the spirit returns back to God who gave it (Eccl. 12:7). Since the spirit is eternal and does not return to dust as the body does, the eternal element remains, no matter what age the physical body may be. When does life begin? It begins at the moment of conception. Why? Conception is the moment the spirit enters the womb. The infant could not live and grow without a spirit. Since the eternal spirit is already there, if a premature death occurs in the womb, the spirit returns to paradise—to God who gave it. It seems that the eternal spirit of the child might mature to a certain level, although we cannot be absolutely certain that it will be the same level for each child.

Despite the tragedy of losing a child through miscarriage or still-birth, the good news is this: That mother—if she remains in covenant with Christ—will see her child again.

CHAPTER 11

How Old Will We
Look in Heaven?

HE BIBLE PROVIDES some interesting facts about the afterlife. When a believer thinks of having a "spirit body," or a "spiritual body," various mental perceptions fill our imagination. Many, I believe, view Scripture through a pair of Hollywood studio glasses. In the secular movie industry, when people die, they transform into a ghostly, semi-transparent, three-dimensional being. Some perceive a person's spirit to be similar to a colorful hologram, with a rainbow of colors glittering from a bodily form. Others imagine a spirit body as the exact replica of the living person who stepped out of their physical body in a glowing form, like a heavenly light bulb.

The Bible gives few examples of what a person *looks like* after the spirit and soul depart from the body. We can, however, use the example of Christ to examine the characteristics of a resurrected body, as Christ was raised from the dead three days after His death.

This might seem simple and unimportant to some, but a resurrected body has hair. For those who have no hair, or like the hair you do have, God will give you a headful of hair at your resurrection. Christ's hair is described as "white like wool, as white as snow" (Rev. 1:14). According to most scholars, Christ was between the age of 33 and 34 when He was crucified. It is not common for a person that age to have white or even gray hair. Some suggest that the physical and emotional shock Christ experienced—from the agony and stress in Gethsemane, where His sweat became blood (Luke 22:44), to His horrible scourging and crucifixion—impacted his body to the point that His hair color may have changed, so that at His resurrection, His hair was completely white.

While medical science cannot explain it, history does record instances of hair turning white suddenly. For example, the hair of condemned prisoners Sir Thomas More and Marie Antoinette is said to have turned white overnight. A medical condition can occur when a person has a mixture of dark and grey (or white) hair. Several things, including severe stress, can cause the dark hair to fall out, leaving only the grey, and thus causing a person to appear they have turned gray suddenly. As a child, I recall a minister who was driving in heavy fog at night and almost hit a moving train. He went into shock, and within one week, his dark hair had begun to turn grey. The bottom line, and the good news for some of you, is that you will have hair in heaven. It might be solid white, but at least you'll have hair!

AGE IN THE BIBLE

In the New Testament we read of "elders" being appointed in churches (Acts 14:23). Throughout the New Testament, the Greek word used sixty-five times for elders is *presbuteros*. This refers to an older male member of the church who assists with various congregational ministries. The word stems from the Greek word *presbus*, meaning *elderly*.

These elders were to be full of faith, wisdom, and the Holy Spirit. If an elder entered full-time ministry and was appointed spiritual leader over a church or a region, he was then called a "bishop" (Titus 1:5-7). The Greek word for bishop is *episkopos*, and in Greek culture this referred to a man who was a ruler, overseer, or superintendent.

In the Old Testament era, within Israel the tribal leaders were considered the elders; at times, additional elders were appointed for leadership. These were to be older men within the congregation who would assist in overseeing various matters within the tribe and the camp. God instructed Moses to appoint seventy elders. The Holy Spirit came upon them to strengthen them in caring for the nation of Israel in the wilderness (Exod. 24:1).

The age of an elder can be debated. In the priesthood, a Levite had to be thirty before he could perform ministry duties at the Temple and the Tabernacle. Even in the United States, the Constitution says that no person can serve as a Senator until they have attained the age of thirty years (Article 1-Section 3). In western culture we do not consider a person an elder at age thirty. However, a level of spiritual maturity is recognized in Scripture at age thirty.

When God formed Adam, he was created a full grown man. There is no indication of how old he was, but because the Torah states that twenty was the age for military service and thirty the age for entering the priesthood, some believe Adam would have been created as an adult between twenty and thirty years of age. We do not know how long Adam lived in the Garden of Eden before he sinned, but we know he was 130 years of age when his son Seth was born (Gen. 5:3). There was also a period of time that Adam was alone before God created Eve (Gen. 2:8-21).

The Apostle John described a scene in the heavenly Temple, in which he saw twenty-four thrones with twenty-four elders sitting upon these thrones (Rev. 4:4). There are twelve references to these elders in Revelation (4:4, 10; 5:5, 6, 8, 11, 14; 7:11, 13; 11:16; 14:13; 19:4). Many scholars believe these men are the twelve sons of Jacob from the Old Covenant, and the twelve apostles of Christ from the New Covenant. There is little description of these men, other than they wear white robes and have gold harps and gold crowns. These elders worship God and the Lamb throughout the entire apocalypse, and there is also no indication of how old they appear.

How old a person appears is a matter of perception. We all have seen individuals who were forty, but who had abused their bodies and looked sixty-five or older. We have also seen men and women in their seventies who physically appear to be twenty years younger. Skin color, wrinkles, hair, and other things have a bearing upon age perception.

Throughout the years, many individuals have encountered a near death experience, or were revived after being declared dead after an accident, massive heart attack, and so forth. Upon arriving in the celestial region, they often see family or close friends who have passed on. At times they will see one of their own children who died, and the child looks the same age he or she did at death. They have described seeing a familiar person who died at a very old age, yet when in this heavenly region, the person looks young.

After reading and researching hundreds of life after death experiences, *no one has ever reported seeing a person in heaven who looks old, regardless of their age when they died.* Most describe the person's appearance as looking as they did on earth between the ages of thirty and forty.

One unique story could explain how your age is determined in heaven. Years ago, while ministering in Indiana, Vonda Bishop introduced me to a man who wanted to tell me an astonishing story. This gentleman shared with me that his wife had passed away from cancer in her 40s, and how it had impacted the family, and especially his oldest daughter. After grieving and crying for her mother, one night the daughter had a dream and saw her mother appear in her bedroom. The mother expressed that her daughter should not grieve anymore, because heaven was far beyond what words can express.

The daughter said she felt such peace and noticed that her mother looked young, healthy and strong—nothing like she appeared before she died. Her mother told her that, when you arrive in heaven, an angel asks how old you want to look. She told the angel that she wanted to look as she did when she was thirty-one. Following this brief incident, the daughter shared this experience with her father. He was so moved that he told his wife's best friend, who had been with her during her suffering and until the time of her death. The friend was shocked, as she had never shared the following story with the family.

The friend said there was a picture of his wife in the house, and in the picture, she was beautiful and healthy. The wife had told the friend, "I hope when we get to heaven that we get to decide what age we want to be. I was thirty-one in that picture, and that's the best I ever looked. I want to look like that when I get to heaven."

In modern culture, a person might live into their seventies or eighties. For those blessed to live long beyond their eighties and into their nineties, by the time they have lived nearly a century, their physical appearance exposes their age. In the days before Noah's flood, men lived longer lives. Adam died at age 930, Methuselah at 969, and Lamech at 777 years (see Genesis 5). How did these pre-flood patriarchs look when reaching their 300th and 400th birthdays? Did they age in the same manner we do today? Did wrinkles cover their faces like a prune? Were their eyes dim? Did bodily functions diminish by the time they were 80, as we see today? Moses died at age 120 and his eyes were not dim, nor had his natural forces diminished (Deut. 34:7). Obviously there is a huge difference between a man who dies at 120 and one who dies at age 969...849 years to be exact.

CHILDREN IN HEAVEN

Opinions differ—even among ministers and scholars—about children in heaven. Some believe that, when a child dies, in heaven they will grow to a mature age and will be young adults when we see them again. However, this contradicts Jesus when he said that children are part of the kingdom of heaven, and their angels continually behold God's face (Matt. 18:10). Others believe there is a special place in paradise for the souls and spirits of infants and children, who will remain as children in the future kingdom.

In 1848, a woman from Berlin, New York named Margareta Davis became sick and fell into a sleep from which she did not awaken for nine days. When she awoke with her full senses, she told of a remarkable journey into heaven. The account was published by Gordon Lindsay in the 1950s in a book titled, *True Visions Beyond the Grave.* In brief, she was carried to heaven by a guardian angel, and she later saw numerous angels that were sent on "errands of mercy." As she observed these angels on assignment, she was drawn to an angel that had ascended from earth to heaven bearing in its arms a small infant spirit. The tiny spirit was being carried into a paradise of peace.

When speaking of children, Christ said that in heaven, "their angels" continually see the face of God. If these children's angels are commissioned on earth to be a guardian and continually watch over a child, then they cannot continually see the face of the heavenly Father. David spoke of these guardian angels when he said that "the angel of the Lord encampeth round about those that fear the Lord and delivers them" (Psa. 34:7). The Hebrew word *encampeth* means to pitch a tent or to camp out. This passage implies an angel that remains in one location for a steady assignment.

If the guardian angel of the child is with the spirit of that child in heaven, then the angel continually sees the face of God. I believe that when an infant or child passes from this life, there is a guardian angel that brings the spirit of the child from earth to heaven. Angels are involved in transporting the spirit of the righteous at the time of death. When the beggar died at a rich man's front door, the angels carried him (his spirit) into Abraham's bosom, to his resting place (Luke 16:22).

As I have traveled the nation over the years, I have met many interesting people with unusual faith-building stories. One such story was a family who had a daughter with serious physical birth defects, including the inability to walk. She became sick at age five and was taken to a hospital where the family was called in to see her for the last time. After she was declared dead and the family cleared the room to allow the hospital workers to take the body, their Pastor asked if he could remain for just a few minutes. He was given a short time alone in the room.

What he saw both stunned and frightened him. He watched as a dark being, a shadowy figure shrouded in black, stepped through the wall. In his mind he began to say, "What is this? This cannot be from God, and it cannot touch the spirit of this child!"

No sooner did he think this, than two beams of light like a shaft descended into the room, and immediately the dark figure (which he believed was a death spirit) instantly vanished. The two light beams formed beautiful angelic figures, one on the left and the other on the right side of the child's bed.

Immediately, these angels placed their bright wings under the hospital bed and lifted their wings upward. Their wings lifted the child's spirit from her departed body, and she was literally lying on the wings of two angels as they lifted her up. Her spirit had no deformities. She even looked toward the pastor and smiled as she was carried through the roof by these powerful angels.

Another remarkable story was related on our Manna-fest telecast by a great man of God, Theo Carter, who at the time was an older minister of the Gospel. In 1947, his nine-year old son, Charles Edward Carter, was playing in a road and shooting fireworks, when a man in a truck accidently ran over the lad and killed him. Theo and his wife Thelma were strong believers, but they grieved the loss of their precious son.

Forty-three years later in 1990, Thelma was sent for heart surgery in Louisville, Kentucky. While on the operating table, her heart stopped and doctors could not revive her. They covered her with a sheet and were ready to pronounce her dead and have her body taken from surgery to the morgue. To the shock of the doctors, she came back to life. They family later determined that she had been dead approximately twenty-one minutes.

During this time, she had been in heaven and had a marvelous experience to tell. While her spirit was there, she had seen her nine-year old son, Charles Edward, who looked exactly as he did when he was killed forty-three years prior. He recognized his mother. Charles was also with several saints of God that Thelma and Theo had known during their lifetime and had passed away. Charles informed his mother that he and other children played on the streets of gold. Thelma was amazed that Charles looked the same age and had the same appearance as he did at his death, forty-three years earlier. Thelma noticed a minister who had been good friends with the family on earth. Charles told her, "Mom, he is my guardian angel up here."

Theo Carter, being the father of this lad and the husband of Thelma, was a man of impeccable integrity and holy living, and this story was known among the mountain holiness people in Kentucky.

As I have listened to stories in my travels and read books on this topic, the question arises: Why is it that, when deceased children are seen in a dream, vision, or life-after-death experience, some appear as they did when they passed away, while others appear more grown up? Assuming, when we are escorted by angels into paradise, that we are permitted to select our appearance based upon a certain age, then how could a child know what it would be like to be an adult, if they departed earth as a child? We can use the Bible and personal experiences such a those mentioned to answer some questions, but others will have to be answered when we get to heaven.

THE ROBES IN HEAVEN

The book of Revelation indicates that, once the saints are resurrected and those living are transformed from mortality to immortality, we will first appear with believers from all nations in the massive Heavenly Temple where a "number that no man can number" (Rev. 7:9) will be worshipping God, along with ten thousand times ten thousands and thousands of thousands (Rev. 5:11).

Several times in the Apocalypse, John observed the attire being worn by the saints in heaven as white robes (Rev. 6:11; 7:9, 13, 14). Clearly, John was familiar with this form of dress, as in the ancient Mediterranean world, robes or similar garments had been worn for thousands of years. Robes can be of various colors, but in John's vision, he simply sees white robes. White represents purity and righteousness. For those in contemporary society, the idea of robes is foreign. Throughout the Middle East however, woman and even men in the Gulf States often wear clothing with an appearance similar to robes.

One of the greatest women of God I have ever met is affectionately known as Aunt Bea. She has directed our Daughters of Rachel intercessor team of praying woman since its inception. Bea Ogle is a great prayer warrior and has an ear to hear the Holy Spirit.

Many years ago, after intense prayer, she was lying down to sleep when she had a marvelous experience. Suddenly she was being carried through the roof of her house into the upper atmosphere. All around her in the distance, she saw people rising from different locations into the air. She thought, "This is the return of Christ! The living saints are being caught up to meet the Lord!" She found herself at a gate in heaven, and as it opened, she saw a multitude gathered from all nations in this one location. She knew it was a gathering place, but what she saw astounded her.

She said, "Everyone was wearing the most beautiful white robes. The sleeves went to the wrists and the lower hems went to the person's ankles. They were perfectly tailored for each person and were a bright, almost silky white. Two things stood out that I had never heard the Scripture talk about. I saw a beautiful bright red stripe that came across the right shoulder and into the front of the robe of every person. The second feature was a pomegranate that was sowed on different areas of the garment."

She never asked about the red stripe, but was curious about the pomegranate on each garment. She overheard a voice informing her that the area where the pomegranate was sewn identified *the nation* the person was from. Some were positioned over the right chest and others the left. Some were on a right lower area and others on the left. Still others were on the right arm or the left. All who were from America had their pomegranate sewn over their right chest. Thus, when entering Paradise, you will know the nation the person came from by the location of the pomegranate. In heaven will be a multitude from every nation, kindred, tongue, and people (Rev. 5:9).

This is interesting when considering that, in the days of the wilderness Tabernacle and Temple in Jerusalem, the pomegranate was a holy fruit. The royal garments of the high priest contained an ephod with a border of golden bells and embroidered pomegranates between each bell (Exod. 28:33-34).

When Solomon constructed the holy Temple in Jerusalem, he placed two very large columns at the entrance of the doors to the Holy Place; the right pillar was named Jacinth and the left was named Boaz (1 Kings 7:21), who was Solomon's great-great-great-grandfather. On the capitals of the pillars were two hundred pomegranates, set in rows all around (1 Kings 7:19-20).

In rabbinical tradition, there are said to be 613 deeds and commandments the Jews must follow in the Torah. This is said to match the 613 seeds found in a mature pomegranate. With both the Biblical information and tradition surrounding the pomegranate, the red fruit represents the Word and Law of God, that when obeyed through the New Covenant, imparts eternal life with Christ.

When Bea asked my thoughts on the red stripe across the right shoulder of each robe, I immediately thought of two significant narratives of a red thread. The first was the law of the Day of Atonement when, according to Jewish history, three scarlet threads were used during the Atonement ritual. The high priest marked the goat for the Lord by tying a red thread around the goat's neck. The other goat, called the scapegoat, had a red thread tied to its right horn. A third thread that was nailed to the doors of the Temple would supernaturally turn white once the scapegoat died in the wilderness, thus representing that Israel's *sins were forgiven.*

The second story that involved a red threat was when Rahab, the harlot from Jericho, was instructed to tie a red cord in her window as a sign of her new faith in the Hebrew God. This would guarantee that she and her family would be protected when the Hebrew men destroyed the city. The scarlet thread was a mark of faith and identification with the God of the covenant (Josh. 2:18). Thus the red thread on the saints' robes could mark those in heaven, identifying them as covenant followers of Christ.

IN SUMMARY

Another question people ask is: Will we maintain the same weight in heaven? Since our physical weight on earth is generally due to factors such as the number of calories we consume, and since most people put on weight as they get older and their metabolism slows down, I am going to assume that people will not be overweight in heaven. I do not believe we will have excess pounds when we get our glorified bodies, since the soul and spirit are not affected by natural food. The spirit is fed with the Word of God. So the good news is, no more worrying about your weight.

I know of not one older person whose body has aged and whose bones are brittle, eyes dim, and skin wrinkled, who given the choice, would not love to go back to their youth and be thirty again. Thus, when given the opportunity to select their age for eternity, many would choose their early thirties because that was a prime age for them.

On the other hand, a child who departs this life would have no reason to choose to be a grown up, as they have no concept of life or appearance as an adult. Heaven is made up of children. Why would God take the spirit of a child and suddenly have the spirit enter paradise as an adult? What would be the purpose for this, when those who have lost a child on earth are longing to be with them again one day in heaven?

When we consider the answers to many of the questions we have about heaven and eternity, I think we all will agree on one thing. There is much more to look forward to in heaven than you and I ever can imagine!

CHAPTER 12

What Food Will We
Eat in Heaven?

SOME BELIEVERS HAVE a perception that once they receive their new resurrected bodies, there will be no need to eat or drink, since eating is presently a natural function required to sustain physical life on earth. The Bible explains that fasting (total abstinence from food) is a powerful spiritual weapon that clears the mind and draws the human spirit closer to God. A person can survive, perhaps for weeks, without food. But we must have water within three days (some have survived up to a week) or we will experience dehydration, which leads to death. After a long fast, the person must return to eating gradually so the body can return to a normal state.

Does God ever eat? What about the angels in heaven? Do they require food? If so, is it spiritual nourishment, or does it provide strength for the spirit? The answer can be discovered in the Bible.

Look at Adam. The first man was created and personally formed by God, and was given an entire garden to enjoy. God provided plants and trees with every type of fruit for Adam and his descendants to enjoy. God instructed Adam:

> "And God said, "See, I have given you every herb that yields seed which is on the face of all the earth, and every tree whose fruit yields seed; to you it shall be for food."
>
> – GENESIS 1:29 (NJKV)

This instruction was given before Adam and Eve sinned and discovered they were now subject to death and would one day return to the dust of the earth. In fact, one tree, the tree of life, was the sustaining force in maintaining life, strength and health for the couple in the garden. Fruit from the forbidden tree of the knowledge of good and evil would bring a slow death when eaten. The couple had certainly eaten from the plants and trees in the garden, chiefly the tree of life—a location God chose daily to commune with Adam. Man was a spirit living in a physical body that required food to survive.

When Israel was punished and wandered in the desert for forty years, one would have to question how an estimated three million people could be fed for about 14,400 days. The answer: They ate bread from heaven. For six days a week and for one generation (forty years), each morning the people collected a white, round wafer that had an oily texture and tasted like honey (Exod. 16:4, 31; Num. 11:7). This manna was a product of heaven and David noted that "man did eat angel's food" (Psa. 78:25), or in Hebrew, "food of the stony and mighty ones."

Christ recalled Israel's wilderness experience, and when speaking of the Hebrew fathers who ate manna, Christ said that "He (God) gave them bread from heaven to eat" (John 6:31). Heavenly manna is also mentioned in Revelation, in Christ's message to the church at Pergamos, when He promised that in heaven, the overcoming believer will "eat of the hidden manna" (Rev. 2:17). Thus manna is a food that is eaten in heaven.

Once the dead in Christ have been raised and those alive at Christ's return have been transformed from a mortal to an immortal (eternal) living being, will a resurrected body require food? And if so, what can we eat?

Perhaps the best example is found in two narratives of Christ. When the Savior was with His disciples for the Passover supper, Christ took the bread and the fruit of the vine and blessed it, then broke the bread and gave it to His disciples. They dipped the bread in the cup and partook of, what was to Christ, a New Covenant meal. Toward the conclusion Christ reminded them, "I will not drink henceforth of this fruit of the vine, until that day I drink it new with you in my Father's kingdom" (Matt. 26:29). The Father's kingdom is the kingdom of heaven as revealed in John's apocalyptic vision.

The only meal alluded to in heaven is the Marriage Supper of the Lamb mentioned in Revelation 19:9. Using the ancient Jewish wedding as imagery, this Marriage Supper will be the moment where Christ will seal His covenant with His heavenly bride, and once again drink from the cup. I say this because, at the Jewish Seder, there are four cups used with the fourth being called the "cup of consummation." At the Marriage Supper, the resurrected saints will partake of a festive celebration which will include food and drink. So we see that a resurrected body does not prevent a person from eating.

When Christ was raised from the dead, He had a body of flesh and bone; He was not just a glorified spirit. The apostle John recorded that Christ met His disciples at the Sea of Galilee, where Peter caught 153 fish in his net. Afterwards they sat down by a fire and Jesus said, "Come and dine" (John 21:12). This meal consisted of bread and fish (21:13). John does not record that Christ ate, but that He fed the disciples; others assume Christ did eat with His disciples. Whether He did or not has no bearing upon the fact that Christ will eat and drink again in the kingdom.

Fruit Trees in Heaven

Earth, especially the Garden of Eden, was created as a reflection of God's heavenly paradise. The garden included trees, with the most important being (as we have already established) the tree of life. This tree is referred to three times in the book of Revelation (2:7; 22:2, 14). We are told that twelve types of fruit grow on this tree, but we do not know what types of fruit. However, we will eat at least twelve different types of fruit when we are in heaven.

While man lived in Eden, there is no record of him eating any type of meat. Over 1600 years later, after Noah's flood, God spoke of the birds of the air and the fish of the sea being "meat" (food) for man. God did say, however, "But you shall not eat flesh with its life, *that is,* its blood" (Gen. 9:2-4).

Hundreds of years later, the Passover was established and a lamb was roasted and eaten by each Hebrew family. When the Tabernacle and the Temple were constructed, the many animal sacrifices served a dual purpose—as both a sacrificial offering and as food for the thousands of priests. This process continued until the destruction of the Temple in AD 70.

In heaven, there will be no meat offerings, and I believe that no meat will be eaten. I say this, not because God is a vegetarian, as obviously there were thousands of offerings of lambs, rams, bulls and birds offered on the brass altar. I say this because there is no flesh and blood in heaven—only spirits and spirits of just men made perfect. Second, there is no death in heaven, and cooking lamb chops or a T-bone steak would require the death of a flesh and blood creature.

When the saints leave heaven and return to earth to rule with Christ for a thousand years, a new and enlarged Temple will be constructed in Jerusalem. In Ezekiel chapters 44 through 48, the prophet provides a detailed description of an order of sacrifices to be offered on specific days and seasons each day, week or month. Christian scholars often criticize these passages of prophecy, as they imply that these animal sacrifices are linked with sin offerings, and Christ, being the final sacrifice, would not require a lesser sin offering in His own temple.

However, these offerings are in no way connected to the resurrected believers ruling with Christ. They are part of the worship requirement for those who survived the great tribulation and are repopulating the earth. They are a memorial offering, and they possibly will provide food for the many priests who will minister full-time at the Temple.

During the one-thousand-year reign of Christ, there will be special trees grown in Israel that will be used for medicinal purposes by those living on the earth:

> "Along the bank of the river, on this side and that, will grow all kinds of trees used for food; their leaves will not wither, and their fruit will not fail. They will bear fruit every month, because their water flows from the sanctuary. Their fruit will be for food, and their leaves for medicine."
>
> – EZEKIEL 47:12 (NKJV)

The word medicine in this verse refers to a remedy for some disease or affliction. The saints have no need for healing, as our new bodies will be exempt from all infirmities, plagues, or sicknesses. However, the tribulation survivors will still be in physical bodies and will require treatment for sicknesses or any type of infirmity that may attack them. These trees will serve as both food and physical remedies.

CHAPTER 13

What Will We Remember in Heaven?

There is a chasm of difference between the death of a *righteous* and an *unrighteous* person. I have attended funerals (I call them home-goings) of righteous believers who departed this life filled with faith and anticipation. Months before my father passed, I asked him what he thought it would be like to pass from this life to the next. He paused before he replied, "I think the experience will be glorious."

At his home-going, the atmosphere at the T.L. Lowery Foundation Center was one of sadness for the family, who already missed his jovial smile and that slightly raspy voice that could pierce heaven with prayer. Yet joy prevailed over our sorrow, knowing the believing loved ones who remained on earth would, in the future, join him again in the eternal City of God.

Conversely, the death of a known sinner or rejecter of the Gospel has a very different feel, as there is often a somber chill permeating the atmosphere. At times one discerns an uncomfortable silence that numbs the air, and few smiles break across faces. Good things might be said about the departed person's life—that he was a good father, that he worked hard, that people in the community liked him—but it is impossible for the Biblically knowledgeable to rejoice, knowing that the personal life of the departed was contrary to every Biblical commandment, and that the person very likely left this life without a redemptive covenant.

When a redeemed soul is transported from *earth life* to *eternal life*, we read:

"Precious in the sight of the Lord is the death of His saints" (Ps. 116:15). Solomon wrote, "The memory of the righteous is blessed, but the name of the wicked will rot." (Prov. 10:7). Much is said about the departure of the unrighteous:

> "His remembrance shall perish from the earth, and he shall have no name in the street"
>
> — JOB 18:17

> "The face of the LORD is against them that do evil, to cut off the remembrance of them from the earth."
>
> — PSALMS 34:16

> "Cast away from you all the transgressions which you have committed, and get yourselves a new heart and a new spirit. For why should you die, O house of Israel? For I have no pleasure in the death of one who dies, says the Lord God. Therefore turn and live!"
>
> — EZEKIEL 18:31-32

Long after a righteous person has departed, people still have pleasant memories of them. Their good deeds are remembered and they are missed by their family, who anticipate seeing them again. The unrighteous, however, leave no fragrance of pleasant memories on earth when their physical existence ceases.

Take, for example, the following people, and focus on the first thought that comes to your mind when you hear their names. We know what we think of dictators such as Adolph Hitler or Joseph Stalin. After 1900 years, those familiar with church history recall the violent escapades of the schizophrenic Roman Emperor Nero. The name Judas Iscariot is connected to one word—betrayal—after nearly two thousand years.

When we consider the historical memories attached to wicked men such as these, we think of death, destruction, betrayal, and persecution. No pleasant thoughts, kind words, or special anniversaries celebrate their honor. Their names are dishonored, and their graves, if they exist, are seldom visited. The memories of wicked men are cursed by those who endured life under their control.

In your own bloodline, if a sibling or relative who is now departed was violent, abusive, unforgiving and continually angry, there is something within the hearts of the surviving relatives that desires for those negative and often troubling memories to fade like fog in the sun, as family and friends move forward to fulfill their remaining days on earth. There is a reason for this mental separation. Without it, an emotionally wounded person has a difficult time healing, as the abuse and hatred replay over and over in the mainframe of their minds. These terrible memories plant seeds of despondency that birth the fruit of depression.

Also, for those living in a redemptive covenant, the thought of a loved one being separated from God eternally is a heavy weight for the conscience to bear. Only the Holy Spirit can bring comfort in such instances and cause a believer to move forward with their own assignments and destiny.

MEMORY IN HEAVEN

The question has often been asked, "Will I know my loved ones in heaven, or will I know if a family member died lost, once I do not see them there?" The narrative of the transfiguration of Christ may hold a clue. Christ invited Peter, James, and John for a secret meeting on a mountain with two of Israel's most celebrated prophets: Moses and Elijah. The day waxed long and the journey up the huge hill stretched the physical strength of the three disciples and they fell asleep on top of the hill. When they awoke, Elijah and Moses were standing with Christ, speaking to Him of His future death in Jerusalem. Elijah had been transported alive in a chariot of fire, about 700 years prior (2 Kings 2). Moses had died 1,500 years prior, and his body was secretly buried by God Himself in the valley below Mount Nebo, in what is today the country of Jordan (Deut. 34:5-7).

Thus, Elijah was brought out of the third heaven for this encounter, and the spirit of Moses was brought up from Abraham's Bosom, a subterranean world under the earth's crust, where the departed souls of the righteous once rested before the resurrection of Christ (Luke 16:19-31). Moses was brought up from the underworld of Sheol, and Elijah was brought down from the upper region of heaven.

When Peter awoke, he immediately recognized both Moses and Elijah, without anyone telling him who they were. There were no paintings, etchings, photographs, or known images of these two prophets, thus Peter's ability was through *spiritual discernment* from the Holy Spirit that quickened his understanding and enabled him to identify these two men (Luke 9:28-36). This may explain how believers will recognize the saints of old and one another in heaven, without being formally introduced. We are told that God knows the names and number of all the stars (Psalms 147:4), and a detailed count of every hair on our head (Matt. 10:30). Thus eternal knowledge far surpasses human intellect, and outside of the human limitations, the human spirit will advance in spiritual understanding, once we become "the spirits of just men made perfect" (Heb. 12:23).

One New Testament verse written by Paul answers the question, "Will we know one another in heaven?" In 1 Corinthians 13, the apostle explains that spiritual gifts designed to edify the church are only temporary, and useful until the return of Christ (1 Cor. 13:10). He emphasized the eternal characteristic of love that will abide forever. He then gave these words, revealing how we would be known when "that which is perfect (Christ in His kingdom) comes."

> "For now we see in a mirror, dimly, but then face to face. Now I know in part, but then I shall know just as I also am known."
>
> – 1 CORINTHIANS 13:12

Presently, our knowledge is "in part," or we would say that we have "partial knowledge." When we are face-to-face with the one who is perfect, that is Christ, then the partial understanding will be done away with and we will have complete knowledge. All of your whys will be answered, such as, "Why was my family member not healed? Why did my child pass away early and not live out his life? Why did I suffer so much? Why were some of my prayers not answered?"

Paul points out that he will be known as he is known. The Greek word *known* is *epiginosko*, which means, "to recognize and become fully acquainted with; to acknowledge." This ability in eternity to recognize a person whom you know and even those you have never met is part of the activity of the Holy Spirit. We read:

> "The Spirit Himself bears witness with our spirit that we are children of God."
>
> – ROMANS 8:16

The 1611 King James translation says the Spirit *beareth* witness, a word in Greek derived from a compound word that means a co-learner, or a fellow disciple. The word *witness* is used in a court setting to describe a person who has some type of evidence that will either justify or condemn the one being prosecuted. It is the Holy Spirit Himself who correctly identifies true believers in any gathering. This inner "witness" of the Holy Spirit has occurred many times in my personal life. I might be in a mall or a restaurant, and see a person I have never seen before or personally met, and know in my spirit they are a believer. It had nothing to do with their outward appearance, or any activity occurring, but like a magnet the Holy Spirit gravitates toward other believers.

There are nine gifts of the Holy Spirit referred to in 1 Corinthians 12:7-10. These nine are divided into three distinct categories; mind gifts, power gifts, and vocal gifts. The three mind gifts are word of wisdom, word of knowledge, and discerning of spirits. When my father was living, I often saw these three gifts operate during his pulpit ministry. At times, the Holy Spirit would reveal minute details concerning a person's family or situation, yet Dad had no personal knowledge of the situation. The Holy Spirit released the word of knowledge, and also at times the discerning of the types of spirits attacking the individual.

Jesus operated in these gifts when, by the Spirit, He saw Nathanial sitting under a fig tree, even though He was not physically present to actually see the incident (see John 1:44-50). Christ also discerned the root cause of a sickness when he prayed for a woman who had been suffering for eighteen years. She was never prayed for by her rabbi or released from her physical weakness until Christ identified the culprit as a "spirit of infirmity" (Luke 13:11-12).

The Holy Spirit sparks the flame of knowledge in the mind of a believer, and the human spirit is the spiritual antenna that connects the earthly with the heavenly. We presently see through a dull mirror with limited knowledge and understanding, but once the human spirit is outside the limitations of the body (through death or through the catching away of the believer—1 Thess. 4:16-17), our knowledge vault will be unlocked and amazing insight will be released.

Paul spoke about having the gift of prophecy and the ability to understand all mysteries (1 Cor. 13:2). This fullness of understanding all mysteries will never occur while we are on earth, living in our bodies of flesh, but will be released outside of the body.

Clearly, in heaven we will recognize family members, friends, former church members, and anyone we personally knew on earth. The question then arises, will we have knowledge of any family members who died in an unregenerate spiritual condition without Christ, and are separated in the chambers of Hades and Sheol? There is little Scriptural teaching on this thought, but there are some points that can be made related to how God forgets.

One of the great mysteries of God's nature is His ability to *know all things,* and yet *choose to forget* other things. How can a God with unlimited knowledge, who designed your body in the womb (Psalms 139:13-16; Jeremiah 1:5) and counts the number of your days, also know all the sins you have committed; but once you confess your sins, ask forgiveness, and enter into a redemptive covenant, choose to forgive and forget your transgressions? Yet the Bible indicates this does occur:

> "I, even I, am He who blots out your transgressions for My own sake; and I will not remember your sins."
>
> – ISAIAH 43:25

The word *remember* in Hebrew is *zakar* and means to *mark, remember or mention.* Thus the Lord will never and can never *bring up any* sin that has been forgiven and cleansed by the blood of Christ. God spoke to Jeremiah that if Israel would repent and receive His law in their hearts, He would "remember their sins no more" (Jer. 31:34). It is uncertain if not remembering means that God totally erases the memory of your sins from His mind, or if He simply refuses to permit the past sins ever to *be brought up* again, as the word remember (zakar) can allude to not mentioning something. Forgiveness is the reason for the death and resurrection of Christ.

We must retain memory of events which transpired on earth, because we will be judged on things we have done. Otherwise, when those earthly deeds are presented at the judgment seat of Christ in heaven, we would have no comprehension of the things upon which we are being judged. This judgment, called the bema, occurs in heaven (Rev. 11:18) and is exclusively for those who died in Christ or who were living and caught up to be with the Lord (1 Thess. 4:14-17). Paul wrote:

> "But why do you judge your brother? Or why do you show contempt for your brother? For we shall all stand before the judgment seat of Christ. As I live, says the Lord, every knee shall bow to Me, and every tongue shall confess to God. So then each of us shall give account of himself to God. Therefore let us not judge one another anymore, but rather resolve this, not to put a stumbling block or a cause to fall in our brother's way."
>
> – ROMANS 14:10-13 (NKJV)

> "For we must all appear before the judgment seat of Christ, that each one may receive the things done in the body, according to what he has done, whether good or bad."
>
> – 2 CORINTHIANS 5:10-11 (NKJV)

This judgment is based on the *good or bad* we did while in our body, meaning when we lived on earth. Paul warned against having contempt or disregard toward fellow believers, and he warned that God will judge us for creating a stumbling block for others. Christ said we will account for our words, and our own mouth will seal our guilt or justify our actions.

> "But I say to you that for every idle word men may speak, they will give account of it in the Day of Judgment. For by your words you will be justified, and by your words you will be condemned."
>
> – MATTHEW 12:36-37

These verses indicate that all believers will remember people they dealt with on earth, words they spoke to them, and how they treated each person. At the judgment, books are opened which contain detailed records of words and actions, and each person will be judged based on the information in each book. It is unclear who compiled these books; however, there is a belief that angels are assigned to individuals, and it is their reports of human events that make up the details of each person's life.

For example, the Italian centurion Cornelius feared God, prayed always, and gave charity to the poor. An angel of the Lord came to him saying that his prayers and giving (alms in the King James Version) had come up before God as a memorial. This indicates that heavenly records were kept, which detailed this man's prayers and charitable contributions. Perhaps this angel was the messenger assigned to the house of Cornelius and was sent from God to reveal to him that God was noting his faith, prayers, and giving.

When the Lord and two angels showed up at Abraham's tent, these three men were on a heavenly assignment to prepare Lot for the destruction of the city of Sodom. The two angels, whose appearance was as human men, were to journey to Sodom and investigate reports coming from the distressing cries of people in the city. We read:

> "And the Lord said, "Because the outcry against Sodom and Gomorrah is great, and because their sin is very grave, I will go down now and see whether they have done altogether according to the outcry against it that has come to Me; and if not, I will know."
>
> — GENESIS 18:20-21

The cries of innocent victims and abused individuals ascend to the ears of God, and these cries can move angelic messengers to bring judgment against the abuser. Jesus told us that children have an angel in heaven that continually beholds the face of God (Matt. 18:10). He warned against offending a little one, and if you are the offender, it would be better to tie a milestone around your neck and throw yourself into the sea.

At the Judgment Seat of Christ, each person being individually judged will have full recall of past words and actions that will be presented by Christ himself. Good will be rewarded, while anything that is not good can cause a person to lose any eternal reward, including the possibility of losing your crown (Rev. 3:11).

Christ warned His critics and unbelieving enemies that, at the judgment (this would be the great white throne judgment, Rev. 20:11-15), it will be more tolerable for the wicked men of Sodom than for the religious leaders who mocked and blasphemed Christ (Matt. 10:15; 11:23). Christ noted that the men in Nineveh and the queen of the south would testify against Christ's generation, because they saw the Messiah and His miracles and refused to believe (Matt. 12:41-42). This indicates that revealed and known information that dates back thousands of years will be recalled at the future judgment. Thus up until the great white throne judgment, memories of the past will be maintained in the memory bank of all humans.

WHEN YOUR MEMORY IS ERASED

There is one Scripture that seems to contradict this thought of retaining our earthly memory in heaven:

> "For, behold, I create new heavens and a new earth: and the former shall not be remembered, nor come into mind."
>
> – ISAIAH 65:17

Clearly, at the Judgment Seat of Christ, which takes place in heaven during the middle of the earthly great tribulation (Rev. 11:18), there will be recall of people, places and events. This recall will continue as we rule on earth for a thousand years with Christ. At the end of the thousand years, the great white throne judgment will occur (Rev. 20:11-15). Following this, after death and hell are assigned to the lake of fire, God creates a new heaven and a new earth (Rev. 21: 1). Once the Holy City, the New Jerusalem, comes down from God out of heaven, the Lord will make "all things new" (Rev. 21:5).

This is when the *former things* (life on the previous earth) *will no longer be remembered*. During the thousand-year reign of Christ on earth, all resurrected believers will begin a new life of ruling and reigning with Christ. It is a mystery to comprehend how our past earthly relationships will continue, since we love our family and children, and want to spend time with them. I believe one of the main reasons why, when we step into eternal timelessness, the past things will never enter our mind, is to *delete the memory* of anyone from our bloodline *who died without Christ's redemptive covenant.* It would not be a joyful New Jerusalem if, for ages to come, our minds were upon those eternally separated from us. Also, life has many disappointments, negative memories, and bad circumstances that need to be erased from our memory vault.

Memory is a God-given gift that enables humans to recall valuable or needed information and store images in the brain. Memory serves both a practical and spiritual function, and enables us to recall the words, promises, and Commandments of God. The Almighty continually said to Israel, "Remember the Sabbath..." (Exod. 20:8); "Remember to do all the commandments..." (Num. 15:39); "Remember how the Lord led you..." (Deut. 8:2), indicating the necessity of a good memory.

Eventually we will make an exit from this planet. In 2 Peter 1:13-15 (KJV), we read:

> "Yea, I think it meet, as long as I am in this tabernacle, to stir you up by putting you in remembrance; Knowing that shortly I must put off this my tabernacle, even as our Lord Jesus Christ hath showed me. Moreover I will endeavor that ye may be able after my decease to have these things always in remembrance."

Peter called his physical body "my tabernacle" (v-14). In Greek, the word *tabernacle* used here is *skenoma*, referring to *a tent*. Paul used the word tabernacle to refer to the physical body (2 Cor. 5:1, 4); and during the transfiguration, when Peter spoke of building three tabernacles (Matt. 17:4), he used the word *skenos*. The idea is that as a tent does not last forever, so the physical body does not last forever. The "putting off of my tabernacle," referred to Peter's death, which did happen shortly after he wrote this epistle. He desired that, after his death, believers would continue to remember these things.

The word *decease* (v. 15) in Greek is *exodos*, meaning "the road out." This word in Greek is used in the New Testament, once where Moses and Elijah spoke of the Lord's death (decease, Luke 9:31) and in Hebrews 11:22, which refers to the departure of Israel out of Egypt, called the Exodus. Our death is literally an exodus, similar to the great departure of the Hebrew nation out of Egypt to their Promised Land.

THE MEMORY OF THE SINNER

Luke recorded a story where Christ spoke of a beggar and a rich man, both who died about the same time. The rich man found his soul and spirit in hell and the beggar was carried by the angels into a compartment for the righteous, called Abraham's bosom. In hell, the former rich man could recall his past life and the fact that he had five brothers still living on earth—all of whom he wanted to warn not to come to this terrible place. The memory of this selfish man was just as alert in the afterlife as when he lived on the earth.

All lost and deceased humanity who are confined in the chambers of the underworld also retain their memories while in confinement. They will remember their deeds at the time of the great white throne judgment, when death and hell deliver up the dead which were in them (Rev. 20:13). Memories of their past actions must be recalled at the judgment, because they must answer for the deeds of their life and words of their mouth, as they are judged according to their works (Rev. 20:12).

After this judgment, we read where death and hell are cast into the lake of fire, a final place of eternal punishment. This is called the "second death" (Rev. 20:14). Some have viewed the statement, "second death," to indicate that at this point, all those in hell will be consumed and annihilated once and for all, thus they will completely perish. When teaching this doctrine, some point out that Christ said it was not His will that any perish, indicating that in the end, the sinners in the lake of fire would completely be consumed to ashes and cease to exist.

First, consider the condition of the lost soul at this moment. They are in a compartment known as hell. Christ was clear that hell has fire and is a place of torment and punishment (Matt. 5:22; 13:42, 50; Mark 9:43-49). Some souls have been confined in this region for hundreds and even thousands of years. Yet, their spirits and souls have not been consumed, and they still exist. We read that the devil, the beast, and the false prophet are tormented in the lake of fire day and night, forever and forever (Rev. 20:10). The punishment is eternal. Simply, forever means forever.

When Christ said He did not want anyone to "perish," the word does not refer to being annihilated or to disappear, but to *destroy, to die, or to lose*. When a person dies in a horrible fire, we say they perished in the fire. Christ is indicating that He does not want anyone to experience the second death, or the second separation from Him and our Heavenly Father. The first death was the soul and spirit being cast into hell, and the second death is being expelled into the lake of fire.

It is unclear if the sinner's memories of the past continue *once they are confined in the lake of fire,* although Luke 16 tells us the rich man was aware of his family members on earth when he was tormented in hell. If I were you, I would ensure my eternal destiny by entering into the redemptive covenant with Christ. He alone has made a plan of escape from eternal death and provided the way for eternal life. There is nothing appealing about the idea of spending eternity in the same location as Satan, his fallen beings, and unrepentant sinners.

To me, the saddest aspect of being eternally separated from God is not just the darkness, loneliness, torment, and thoughts of what could have been. It is also the fact that I would never again see my wonderful wife and children, never love on them, or spend time laughing and playing with them. It is the thought of knowing that the time would come when their memory of me would be completely erased.

Friend, it is not worth spending eternity lost and separated from God and the family you love. Eternity together should be your ultimate and final destination.

CHAPTER 14

What Language is Spoken in Heaven?

W HEN JOHN SAW the massive gathering of redeemed multitudes in heaven, he said they were from "every kindred, and tongue, and people, and nation" (Rev. 5:9). This phrase is repeated in chapter 7 and marks the tribulation multitude from "all nations, kindred, people, and tongues" (Rev. 7:9). This same phrase is found in Revelation 14:6, when John spotted an angel coming down to earth preaching the everlasting gospel to the people on earth, out of "every nation, kindred, and tongue, and people" (Rev. 14:6).

Summing up this phrase, individuals from every ethnic group and nation on earth will be represented in heaven. I have often wondered how we will communicate with one another in heaven, considering that different nations speak different languages. What will be the language of heaven? My primary language is English, and when I pray with my "understanding," I pray in English. Prayers of people from cultures around the world are spoken in their language—Spanish, Portuguese, Russian, and so on. When we arrive in heaven, how can we communicate with different nations of believers? Will we speak our own languages, or are language barriers broken as we speak and worship in one tongue?

In the beginning when God created Adam, the first man fellowshipped every day with God at the tree of life. Obviously they had some form of verbal communication that was known to both Adam and God, as Adam named all of the animals. After eating from the forbidden tree, God entered the garden and rebuked Adam for hiding among the fig leaves (Genesis chapter 3). Although Adam was expelled from the center of the Garden of Eden, he retained his ability to communicate and passed the same language he spoke to his sons (Cain, Abel and Seth). Seth, the righteous seed, passed the original form of communication on to the first ten generations from Adam to Noah (see the ten men listed in Genesis 5).

A major language shift occurred approximately 339 years following Noah's flood, when the descendants of Noah's three sons constructed a massive high-rise called the tower of Babel (Gen. 10:10; 11:4). The post-flood generations were united with one language and believed they were unrestrained in their ability as long as they remained in unity. The Lord interrupted their unity by collapsing their tower and suddenly dividing their one language into many different dialects. Instantly, these men could communicate only with those who spoke the same dialect. This brought confusion and abandonment of their plans, and the event has been called the Babel effect or the confusion of tongues. Once the single language was divided, each person understood only their own tongue. This event was a supernatural moment, as the text indicates that "God confounded the language of all the earth" (Gen. 11:9).

Those who study languages have noted that certain words are similar in numerous languages, which indicates that all languages stem out of one original language. They also note that the Semitic languages of the Mediterranean and early Mesopotamian area (the land of ancient Babel) contain some of the oldest languages in the world.

Moving from Babel in the land of Shinar (Gen.1) to Jerusalem and the Festival of Pentecost (Acts 2:1-4), another linguistic miracle occurred. Christ's disciples, many whom were uneducated Galileans, were suddenly infused by the power of the Holy Spirit and began speaking in new tongues, which were actually known languages of that day. Sixteen different dialects were spoken that day (see Acts 2:7-11). Jews who were visiting Jerusalem from surrounding nations understood the words these men were fluently speaking as the languages of their respective nations. This was a sign of Christ's resurrection given to devout Jews living in Jerusalem and to those Jews participating in the festival (Isa. 28:11-12; 1 Cor. 14:21-22).

This new gift to speak in heavenly or earthly languages (called "the gift of the Holy Spirit" - Acts 2:38) enabled the believers to speak in languages they had never studied. This is called in Greek "glossolalia", and is a supernatural impartation that comes through the indwelling of the Holy Spirit. Years following the initial outpouring of the Spirit, Luke recorded the same spiritual manifestation among new believers in Samaria (Acts 8:17), with Paul (Acts 9:17) and with the twelve disciples at Ephesus (Acts 19:1-7).

Paul taught the church at Corinth that there are nine spiritual gifts, three which were vocal gifts: tongues, interpretation and prophecy. The ability to speak in languages that a person has never learned was evident in the church and considered a gift from the Holy Spirit. In his earlier ministry, one noted minister, Dr. Mark Rutland, was supernaturally given the Spanish language, having never studied it, and to this day he can speak and write in the Spanish language. With the gift of "tongues and interpretation," the Holy Spirit provides both the language being spoken and the ability for a believer to understand (interpret) the language (1 Cor. 12:7-10; 1 Cor. 14).

WILL WE KNOW THE LANGUAGE?

In the time of the New Testament, there were three primary languages: Greek, which was at that time the universal language (the New Testament was written in Koine Greek); Latin, which was the language of the Roman Empire; and Hebrew, which was spoken by the Jews in Jerusalem. The Aramaic language was also known throughout parts of Israel, Lebanon and Syria.

When Paul testified of his conversion experience, he revealed that God called his name "Saul, Saul," out of heaven in the Hebrew tongue (Acts 26:14). With Paul being a devout Jew, a Pharisee, and a teacher of the Law, Hebrew would be the natural language he would have spoken in prayer, when reading the Torah, and when attending the Jerusalem synagogue. A form of Hebrew is believed by some to be the original language of God in heaven and in Eden, and continues to be the language of heaven.

When Paul penned his discourse on the superiority of love (see 1 Cor. 13), he referred to speaking in the tongues of men and of angels (13:1). Consider the tongues (languages) of the angels. When angels appear in a dream, vision, or occasionally in human form, they always communicate in the native language of the person with whom they are speaking. An angel would not appear to a minister who speaks only Chinese and communicate to him in English. He will converse in the minister's native tongue. If we speak only English, any angel sent from the Lord will speak in our English language. Even Paul taught that when a minister is teaching in a public setting, he should teach in the language of the listeners, and not speak in an unknown tongue, so that believers may receive knowledge and edification (1 Cor. 14:18-22).

Numerous individuals have claimed to experience heavenly visions, or what Paul would term an "out of the body experience" (2 Cor. 12:2-4). In many instances, the people experiencing these heavenly encounters reveal that some forms of communication were with *thoughts* and not with *words*. In other words, in the spirit realm, communication can occur by the people reading each other's thoughts. In this manner some questions were answered before the entire thought was released from the individual's mind (or soul). This is interesting in light of Isaiah 65:24: "...before they call I will answer; while they are yet speaking I will hear."

In the earthly realm, it requires time to communicate back and forth with someone. However, in the Spirit realm, there are timeless dimensions that we humans have never encountered. If light can travel at 186,000 miles per second, then the speed of thought is much faster. Thus, theoretically, when we are out of our body and operating in a spirit body, time becomes insignificant; therefore, thoughts can be read instantly the moment they are thought.

In heaven, there are several occasions when the four living creatures, the twenty-four elders, or a multitude are praising and worshipping the Lamb (Christ). One of the songs is "Worthy is the lamb that was slain to receive power, and riches, and wisdom, and strength, and honor, and glory, and blessing ..." (Rev. 5:12). John said that "every creature in heaven, on earth, and under the earth" was blessing the Lamb. The word "creature" is Greek and refers to a thing created and can allude, not only to humans, but to the animal kingdom (Rom. 1:25; 8:19-21). The worshippers include those in heaven, those on earth, those under the earth, and even in the sea. How can all nations and creatures from different nations say the same thing, yet John could understand the words of praise from people of every nation?

The simple explanation is that, once we all arrive in heaven, we will be united by one heavenly language that will be imparted to us supernaturally, in the same manner that the single language at the tower of Babel was divided in a moment's time. No learning process was involved with that supernatural event. The miracle of Pentecost also illustrates the breaking of language barriers. The Jewish inhabitants living in Galilee were linked among the nations of the Gentiles, who often spoke the Aramaic or Greek languages (with Hebrew being spoken mainly in Jerusalem). However, "suddenly there was a sound from heaven," and this sound from heaven was manifested when the disciples spoke in new tongues (Acts 2:1-4).

The Holy Spirit is the imparter of the gift of languages and the gift of interpreting languages. When the family of God on earth is united with those in heaven, once we arrive in the heavenly temple in a "moment" (1 Cor. 15:52), there will be no ethnic walls or language barriers.

If we pass away before Christ returns, we might remain among the souls of the nation into which we were born and be linked with them during our wait in Paradise—just as today in Jerusalem, the city is divided into sections where each religious or ethnic group lives and works. Once the family of God is united from both the Old and New Covenants, then we are provided a language, perhaps a form of Hebrew, enabling us to communicate to all people from all nations.

Attempting to explain certain mysteries of heaven reminds me of the statement Luke the disciple penned when Mary realized she was pregnant with the seed of God's Word. Mary didn't understand how this was possible. The angel said, "For with God nothing shall be impossible" (Luke 1:37). What today is unclear in our understanding will be made crystal clear the moment we enter heaven, as Paul wrote:

> "For now we see in a mirror, dimly, but then face to face. Now I know in part, but then I shall know just as I also am known."
>
> – 1 CORINTHIANS 13:12

At Babel, one language was divided into many, and at Pentecost, one group of Galileans spoke many different dialects. This miracle of languages was overseen by the Holy Spirit. Certainly since He knows all earthly tongues, He is qualified and able to impart one heavenly language to all people in heaven. When we return to earth, He is able to give the saints understanding of the earthly dialects spoke by the survivors of the tribulation. The prophet said it this way:

> "For the earth shall be filled with the knowledge of the Lord, as the waters cover the sea."
>
> – HABAKKUK 2:14

The time, knowledge, and language limitations we encounter while living on earth will all be removed in the future. God gives the gift of diverse (different) tongues (1 Cor. 12:10), which allows the Holy Spirit to supernaturally impart languages to the Spirit-baptized believer. In the same manner, the Lord will have no difficulty imparting to His people, all at once, the ability to communicate in any other language, or many languages.

CHAPTER 15

What Those in Heaven Know About Those On Earth

IN THE PRE-CRUCIFIXION dispensation, the righteous were predominantly sons of Adam who followed God's revealed instruction, and from Moses forward, the Hebrew people who maintained a Covenant relationship with God and were made righteous through faith. After they passed from this life, their eternal souls were carried into the underworld to a place called sheol (hades), where they would remain until the promised Messiah would enter this underworld, release them from their underground prison (1 Pet. 3:18-19), and transfer them to the heavenly paradise.

Based on Luke 16, after death both the righteous and unrighteous souls are fully alert and can access memories long after their eternal soul and spirit leaves their bodies. In Christ's narrative, a rich man who died recalled that he was rich in his previous life, remembered that he had abused a sickly beggar, and was still aware that he had five living brothers. The beggar also remembered that during his earthly life, he had been a poor beggar who had died of starvation on the rich man's property. The patriarch Abraham was able to talk with the men, both of whom had died, yet were living in an eternal realm in two separate regions—one in a land of peace and the other in a land of torment (see Luke 16:19-31).

In Hebrews chapter 11, the inspired writer penned a chapter often referred to as the roll call of the heroes of faith. Each name listed is a noted patriarch, king, prophet, judge or woman from the Old Testament era whose faith was the substance for their life's miraculous history. After a brief review of each person's testimony the writer states, "These all died in the faith, not having received the promises, but having seen them afar off and were assured of them, embraced them, and confessed that they were strangers and pilgrims on earth" (Heb. 11:13). After death, these believers became a "cloud of witnesses:"

> "Therefore we also, since we are surrounded by so great a cloud of witnesses, let us lay aside every weight, and the sin which so easily ensnares us, and let us run with endurance the race that is set before us..."
>
> – HEBREWS 12:1

The Greek word in that verse for cloud is *nefos*, meaning a vast mass of clouds. This phrase is a metaphor alluding to the Greek-Roman amphitheater and the stacked tier above tier seating that rose upward like a cloud. In this case, the witnesses are those who have gone before and completed their spiritual race, and who have passed the baton to the next set of runners and are encouraging them to run and finish their own race. This word was also used in classical Greek. Homer, when speaking of the Trojan foot soldiers, referred to them as the "cloud of footmen." At times when a massive multitude of solders were observed, they were called a "great cloud of men." The Greek word for witnesses is *martus*, from a word meaning a judicial witness, and by analogy is also a martyr.

During the Olympics, rows of observers have their eyes glued upon the athletes, ready to encourage and cheer them on to cross the finish line and win the prize. This verse has initiated a controversial idea, and that is those who have gone before us can at times observe our journey, especially those moments of victory when we overcome and celebrate God's blessings and favor. Most scholars believe the writer is simply using the Greek games as an analogy to encourage Christians to remain faithful during their journey, and lay aside any hindrance that is weighing a believer down. Angels may be the key to understanding the contact between the celestial and terrestrial worlds.

Angels Seek Out Sinners

At times certain Scriptures have been quoted and interpreted one way, but a more detailed and careful study can actually open a different and interesting understanding of the verse. In Hebrews, the writer speaks of the assignments of angels, calling them *spirits* and *a flame of fire* (Heb. 1:7). He reminds the reader that the ministry of Christ was far superior to the angels, and that at Christ's birth, He was worshipped by the angels (Heb. 1:6). One of the interesting insights is penned in Hebrews 1:14: "Are they not all ministering spirits, sent forth to minister for them who shall be heirs of salvation?"

This verse is primarily quoted by believers to indicate that angels minister to those who have received Christ, as we are "heirs of God and joint heirs with Christ" (Rom. 8:17). However, the phrase "who shall be heirs" is future tense. Believers are *now* heirs of God and joint heirs with Christ. From another view, there are numerous individuals who are presently not serving Christ and are void of any redemptive covenant. Yet, their family members and friends are continually interceding for their salvation. Years ago I saw this verse in a different light, meaning that angels are sent forth to minister to those who are will soon be won to Christ, or "shall be" (in the future) heirs of salvation.

Imagine a parent or grandparent who for years has consistently interceded for a child, grandchild or loved one, but goes to be with Christ long before they see any evidence of their prayers being answered. Then picture that unconverted loved one eventually repenting and turning to Christ. Will that prayer warrior who now dwells in heaven ever know the miraculous conversion that has occurred on earth? Or will it require waiting until the end of the repentant person's life, when he enters the heavenly kingdom, before the very ones who prayed them into the kingdom will know they made it? Either those in heaven are made aware at the moment of true repentance, or there is a delay in knowing until they join others in heaven.

The good news is that when a sinner repents, there is immediate acknowledgment in heaven. We might assume that the first response is that a heavenly messenger (possibly an angel) records the repentant person's name in a heavenly registry called the Lamb's Book of Life.

During the heavenly judgments, this and other books will be opened and the dead will be judged according to the information recorded in various heavenly books (Rev. 20:12). Christ also indicated that a sinner's repentance initiates a heavenly celebration as we read that there is joy in the presence of the angels (Luke 15:10). The Greek word "presence" literally means, "in the *face* of the angels." The traditional interpretation teaches that the joy comes from the angels as the name of the former sinner is placed in the heavenly registry. After all, throughout the world at the same moment are individuals from all tribes and nations who turn their hearts to God for redemption and mercy, and this would possibly require hundreds or thousands of angels to inscribe names in the Book of Life.

Another possible interpretation is that, when a sinner repents, those believers in heaven whose prayers for the lost souls were continually before God are informed of the sinner's repentance. This news fills them with joy, and they rejoice in the face of the angels. In this case, it would be the angels themselves who make known the name of the sinner who has repented.

Angels are important messengers on earth, and they sometimes connect individuals. During the infant stages of the early church, the devout religious Jews restrained from fellowshipping with gentiles, as most gentiles were pagan, heathen, or idol worshippers. When Cornelius, a God-fearing Italian centurion and gentile was seeking God for a closer walk with Him, an angel of God knew the name of Cornelius. He also identified Peter by name and gave Cornelius the name of the homeowner where Peter was staying—the "house of Simon the Tanner" (Acts 10:1-20). Angels know not only the names of believers and unbelievers, but are also aware when sinners repent.

What else does the celestial world know about man's activities on earth? Biblically, I can comprehend why angels have such knowledge of earth's events, as they serve as God's divine messengers:

> "To them it was revealed that, not to themselves, but to us they were ministering the things which now have been reported to you through those who have preached the gospel to you by the

Holy Spirit sent from heaven--things which angels desire to look into."

– 1 Peter 1:12

What about those who have departed and have lived in the celestial heaven now for centuries? Perhaps they have unlimited knowledge of heavenly realities, but is their information of earth events severed from them, once they dwell in the eternal paradise of God?

KNOWLEDGE FROM ABOVE AND BENEATH

Prior to Christ's death, who was informed in advance or had prior knowledge that Christ must die, and that his death would bring redemption? The first major prophet to fully predict the suffering Messiah was Isaiah, who recorded his vision in Isaiah chapter 53. Three worlds have spiritual knowledge: the world of God (heavenly realm), the world of man (earthly realm), and the satanic kingdom (the dark world). Christ was fully alert to God's plan and the fact that He would suffer, die, and rise again. Toward the end of Christ's ministry, the High Priest Caiaphas informed a secret council that it was necessary that one man (referring to Christ) would die for the sins of the people. From the moment he revealed this to the council, they sought to kill Christ—as though to fulfill the expectations of the prophecy. Oddly, all other leaders of this world were ignorant of the purpose and plan of God through Christ. Paul taught that, had they known, they would have never crucified the Lord (1 Cor. 2:8).

God accurately revealed details of the Messiah's redemptive mystery to the prophets. Psalms 22:16 says his hands and feet would be pierced (the crucifixion). Isaiah was given insight that the Messiah's soul would be made a sin offering (Isa. 53:10); that His soul would be poured out unto death; and that He would be numbered among the transgressors, and bare the sins of many (Isa. 53:12). The sacred Scriptures were replete with unusual signs and indicators that would mark the future Jewish Messiah as Savior and King of the world. Since Christ was aware of these prophetic verses, why then was it expedient for God to send two of Israel's greatest prophets to appear on the mountain of transfiguration and speak with Christ about His future death in Jerusalem?

Matthew, Mark and Luke write of the marvelous transfiguration, indicating there were three apostolic witnesses present: Peter, James and John (Matt. 17:1; Mark 9:2; Luke 9:30). Both Moses and Elijah appeared with Christ, as God's glory overshadowed these three. These two famous prophets spoke with Christ, detailing "His decease that He should accomplish in Jerusalem" (Luke 9:31).

In Moses' day, he received several previews of the Messiah's work and suffering, and inked his revelations on parchments in the Torah. Abraham had offered Isaac in the "Land of Moriah" upon "one of the mountains," a type of God the Father offering Christ in Jerusalem (Gen. 22:1-2). When a ram replaced Isaac on the altar, Abraham called the name of the place "Jehovah-Jirah," and Moses added this statement, "As it is said to this day, in the mount of the Lord it shall be seen" (Gen 22:14). The place where Abraham bound Isaac was in Jerusalem, on what is today called the Temple Mount. Moses, in his day, understood that a sacrifice would be seen on this mountain, and perhaps Moses appeared with Christ to discuss this aspect of His suffering in Jerusalem. There were numerous types and shadows Moses was aware of, such as the unique offering of the red heifer (see Num. 19) and the brass serpent on a pole (see Num. 21:1-9), both of which encoded specific details of the future crucifixion of Christ.

The oddest aspect of Moses appearing to Christ is that the spirits of the departed Old Testament saints were confined in a compartment under the earth where the righteous souls were gathered at death. That would have include Moses, who died at age 120 on top of a tall mountain in Moab called Mount Nebo, on the east side of the Jordan River. After he died, God scooped up his body and personally buried the prophet in an unmarked grave (see Deut. 34). The same valley where Moses was buried was also the area where Elijah was transported alive into heaven in a fiery chariot (2 Kings 2). When standing in the plains and looking toward ancient Moab, one can see the towering mountain of Nebo, where Moses took his last glance at the Promised Land before departing this life.

Some Hebraic teachers believe the transfiguration occurred on Mount Nebo for several important reasons. First, it is on the Moab side, and Moses was not permitted into the Promised Land. By remaining in Moab at the transfiguration, Moses still had not entered the land, thus keeping God true to His Word. Second, both Moses and Elijah, the two prophets at the transfiguration, have the plains of Moab in common; one was buried there and the other was carried into heaven from there. Third, Nebo is an important mountain when viewing the Promised Land. From its heights on a clear day, one can see Jericho, the Mount of Temptation and the Judean Wilderness. On a totally clear day, looking west, one can see the top of the Mount of Olives in Jerusalem.

The point here is, Moses had been dead for about 1,500 years. However, his soul and spirit had been confined, along with generations of other Hebrew souls, in a paradise compartment called the Bosom of Abraham (Luke 16:19-22). This is where righteous, departed souls were held, beginning with the early descendants of Adam and continuing until the time of Christ's descent into the heart of the earth to release these captives.

The Bible indicates that individuals can carry information from this life into the next life. When Biblical prophets died and entered this underground world, they would have known their own Messianic predictions and expectations. All of the Biblical prophets who had passed—Isaiah, Daniel, Ezekiel, Jeremiah, and the minor prophets—were confined together in this one location. Each prophet's entrance into this underworld brought additional insight and updates from earth regarding God's plan and purpose.

The most exciting update must have been from Rabbi Simeon, who saw Christ a few weeks after His birth. Simeon had been promised he would not die until he saw the Messiah, and he passed after holding the infant Christ at the Temple in Jerusalem (Luke 2:25-35). Simeon might have been the first person to die and enter Abraham's Bosom, and announce that he had seen the Messiah!

Over thirty years later, Lazarus, a personal friend of Christ, died and would have remained with the souls in Abraham's Bosom for about four days before Christ raised him from the dead. Lazarus could have relayed marvelous stories of Christ's ministry and miracles, and also confirmed that the Messiah the prophets wrote about had arrived.

Moses came from below, but Elijah would have appeared from above. Elijah's appearance was for more than a discussion about Christ's death. The appearing of Elijah had an astonishing effect on Peter, James and John for the following reasons. First, Elijah and Enoch are the only two prophets to escape physical death and suddenly be transported from earth to heaven (Gen. 5:22-24; 2 Kings 2:11). Note that neither the bodies of Moses nor Elijah were found (Deut. 34:6; 2 Kings 2:11-18).

The disappearance of Elijah was known to devout Jews for centuries, and based upon Malachi 4:5, Elijah the prophet must reappear on earth before the great and dreadful day of the Lord. At Passover, a Jewish tradition is enacted where a child will leave the table and open the front door to see if he or she sees or hears Elijah making his announcement that the Messiah has arrived. When the three disciples saw Elijah, this would have confirmed that Elijah appeared to confirm that Jesus Christ was truly the anticipated Messiah of Israel. John the Baptist, the cousin of Christ, came in the "Spirit and power of Elijah," as he was a forerunner to Christ's ministry. However, Elijah the prophet appeared in personal form with the Messiah. John the Baptist confessed he was not Elijah, but the fulfillment of Isaiah's promise of a "voice crying in the wilderness to prepare the way of the Lord." The real Elijah was assisting Christ in preparing the way for the coming Kingdom that was being preached by both John the Baptist and Christ: "Repent, for the kingdom is at hand"

Moses' knowledge was from *below* and Elijah's knowledge was from *above*. Moses's knowledge came from his own writings and the insight from the prophets. Abraham lived hundreds of years before Moses, and yet when he spoke to the rich man who requested that Abraham send Lazarus from the dead to warn his brothers, Abraham said, "They have Moses and the prophets, let them hear them" (Luke 16:27-29). *Having Moses* refers to the five books that Moses wrote called the

Torah, which Jews were taught to follow. *The prophets* refers to the prophetic books in the Scripture.

How would Abraham know anything about Moses or the prophets, since Abraham lived hundreds of years before Moses and no prophetic books had been written in Abraham's day? His knowledge came over centuries of time, as when the Hebrew people passed, they had information they brought with them into this paradise below the earth!

Prior to Christ's crucifixion, He was praying in Gethsemane and His sweat became as great drops of blood (Luke 22:44). The stress of His coming suffering was so great, He prayed that if it were possible, for God to take this cup (of suffering) from Him (Luke 22:42). When soldiers arrived and Peter cut off the ear of the High Priest's servant, Jesus told Peter to put away his sword. Jesus revealed that He could call twelve legions of angels if needed (Matt. 26:53). There were eleven faithful disciples (Satan was now controlling Judas) and Christ, totaling twelve. One legion could be assigned to each disciple and one for Christ.

Where did this knowledge of twelve legions of angels on standby come from? There are only three possibilities. Either God spoke directly to Christ while Christ was interceding for three hours in the garden; or the angel from heaven who came to Christ during prayer and strengthened Him informed Him (Luke 22:43); or this possibility was made known to Christ at the time Moses and Elijah spoke with Him on the Mount of Transfiguration. This revelation came from above and not from beneath, as with the exception of angels who transported souls to Abraham's bosom, angels are always observed in heaven, or moving in the atmosphere. In the heavenly realm there are no limitations placed upon knowledge and understanding.

Based on biblical events such as the transfiguration and the post-crucifixion resurrection of pre-crucifixion saints, I believe it is possible that those who pass from earth to heaven can reveal information concerning events on earth to those in heaven. However, if our departed loved ones could look from heaven to earth and see everything we are doing, some would be happy and others perhaps would be grieved. They would rejoice over the good things, but be sorrowful over the bad things. Knowledge and information can be released from angels in both the earthly and heavenly realms, and heaven is aware when a sinner repents.

I have known people who had a near-death experience and could look back and see their families on earth. But from Scripture, I do not believe it is a common thing for the Lord to allow someone to continually peer into their former home on earth. Most likely it is a rare event. With the appearance of Moses and Elijah at the Mount of Transfiguration, this was a one-time event that bypassed the normal laws of eternity.

Our concern should not be with the earthly events that can or cannot be seen by family members; instead, it should be that Christ can always see what we do and hear what we say. We must remember that we will answer to Him and not to our loved ones on the day of judgment.

CHAPTER 16

Assignments in Heaven and On Earth

THIS STATEMENT MIGHT come as a surprise to many, but those who have served Christ as Lord and Savior will not be spending *eternity* in heaven. In fact, for all of us New Covenant recipients, our brief visit in heaven is limited to a set time frame (during the great tribulation, unless we die sooner). At the conclusion of the heavenly marriage supper of the Lamb (Rev. 19:9), we will return to earth, where we will live and rule with Christ for a thousand years (Rev. 20:4). When this millennial reign ends, we will enter a no-time zone called eternity, where believers from all ages will live on a new earth and dwell in the Holy City, the New Jerusalem (see Rev. 21 and 22).

When Christ returns for us, the living saints will be changed from mortality to immortality, and the righteous dead will be resurrected (1 Thess. 4:16-17). In a moment's time, we will receive a new, glorified body that will enable us to time travel from one location to another. Just as holy angels can transport themselves from earth to heaven and back to earth with the speed of a blink of an eye, believers will access the same angelic traveling ability in a new immortal body whose molecular structure is presently a mystery. Even the Apostle Paul used the word *mystery* when attempting to explain how the body is changed from a mortal body of death to an immortal one incapable of ever dying again (1 Cor. 15:51-54).

The New Testament indicates there are two groups of believers Christ receives at His coming: those living and those who have died. Those participating in the *dead in Christ resurrection* are men, women and children from all nations, from the early days of the church, to the moment the shofar blast is heard raising the dead. Those who are *living* will be believers from all nations who are actively serving Christ and whose names are written in the Lamb's book of life (Rev. 21:27).

The book of Revelation covers the seven years of the tribulation, from Rev. 4:1 to Rev. 19:21. During these seven years, four different groups will appear in heaven before the throne of God.

The heavenly multitude begins with the Old Testament saints and patriarchs, such as Abraham, Isaac, Jacob, David and so forth, and all of the Covenant people of ancient Israel who followed God's pre-law instruction by walking in the Abrahamic covenant (circumcision). This will include later generations of Hebrews who faithfully followed God's law given to Moses in the Torah. These would primarily be Hebrew believers and later Jews from Judea. The Old Testament multitude includes all righteous individuals who lived as far back as Adam and up to the crucifixion of Christ. These first covenant people followed the spiritual visions and dreams of the patriarchs (Abraham, Isaac and Jacob) that formed the nation of Israel from the Exodus onward.

Not all *Hebrew* people (the name identifying the Israelites from Abraham through the Exodus) followed the Lord. Korah, along with his house and friends, rebelled against Moses. God judged them by opening the earth and bringing these wilderness rebels down into the pit (see Num. 16). Three thousand Israelites died after worshipping the gold calf, and later thousands died when God sent plagues (see Exod. 32). In the Old Testament dispensation, the unrighteous went down into the "pit" and the righteous descended into Abraham's bosom (Luke 16:22-24). The saints from Adam to the crucifixion will be a part of this heavenly multitude.

The next heavenly group will be all saints living on earth who were actively serving Christ when He returns during the great catching away, and all who have died in Christ, identified as the "dead in Christ" (1

Thess. 4:16-17; 1 Cor. 15:51-52). Being *in Christ* was an early church phrase that marked those who had died in covenant with Christ. This phrase was so important to the first century church that, if a believer was slain or martyred, instead of placing their names on the burial tombs, often symbols were used, such as a dove (representing the Holy Spirit), a whale (representing Jonah's resurrection after three days), or simply the words, "In Christ." Those who died in Christ from the time of His resurrection to the time of His return for the church will make up this heavenly assembly, along with saints living at the moment the trumpet of God sounds.

A third group that appears in heaven during the great tribulation are the souls slain or beheaded during the horrible time of tribulation. This group is called a *multitude*, and their numbers are known only to God. Once they are martyred, their spirits are transferred out of their bodies and transported to a heavenly paradise where they are outfitted in white robes and instructed to rest until their fellow believers are slain and brought to heaven (Rev. 6:9-11). These martyrs of the tribulation must be raised, as they will rule with Christ on earth for a thousand years. We are uncertain of when they are raised, but some place their resurrection at the end of the tribulation. Others say they must be present at the marriage supper with Christ and the church (Rev. 19).

The fourth group in this heavenly assembly is a selected Jewish remnant of men, 12,000 from each tribal region of Israel, totaling 144,000 who are supernaturally sealed with a "seal of God" on earth during the first half of the tribulation. These men will be caught up to heaven sometime midway through the tribulation. There is much speculation about why God initiates this sealing and protective covering from the Antichrist for this group of men, all who are unmarried and Jewish. One simple theory is that, throughout history, God has marked a remnant of people and separated them from among others. John identified them as "the (Jewish) first fruits of the Lamb," meaning the first of the Jewish population to receive the Messiah (Rev. 14:4).

These four groups, the Old Testament saints, the New Covenant saints, the 144,000 Jewish men, and the tribulation martyrs will combine as one heavenly assembly to form the kingdom of God on earth, when Christ the Messiah returns to Jerusalem to set up His millennial kingdom.

THE DIFFERENT ASSIGNMENTS

There are three specific locations in which men and women from these various ages will be assigned. They will either be appointed to serve God in *heaven*, in the *millennial reign*, on the *new earth*, or in some instances, all three.

First look at the *144,000 Jews* mentioned in Revelation 7:1-8 and 14:1-4. During the first part of the tribulation, Elijah the prophet appears in Israel as one of the two witnesses (Mal. 4:4-5). During his ministry, these Jewish men are sealed by an angel (messenger) coming from the east. This messenger may be Elijah himself who unites these men under his leadership in the first forty-two months of the tribulation. To this day, each year at Passover, all devout Jews anticipate the appearance of Elijah to announce the arrival of the Messiah (Mal. 4:5). The *seal* that protects them from the Antichrist will be "the Father's name on their forehead" (Rev. 14:1). The Father's name could be numerous compound Hebrew names for God penned throughout the Hebrew Scriptures. However, the sacred name of God is YHVA, transliterated in English as Jehovah. According to Jewish tradition, there is special power concealed in the name of God, pronounced according to some as Yahweh.

These men are "raptured" at mid-point during the tribulation and appear before the throne of God (Rev. 14:5). These will "follow the Lamb wherever he goes" (Rev. 14:4). This implies they will serve Christ, function as ministers in the heavenly temple, and also return to earth with the "armies of heaven" (Rev. 19:14) where they will serve Christ in Jerusalem. Their specific assignments are unknown. However, at the earthly Temple in Jerusalem, there will be a need for hundreds of thousands of workers each day to serve in the temple ministry (see Ezekiel 44-47).

The next group is the *multitudes beheaded* during the tribulation (Rev. 20:4). These appear to be individuals who were unprepared for the return of Christ. According to several parables of Christ, there will be two types of "servants" at this coming: those who are *profitable* and those who are *unprofitable*. This has no reference to money (or profit), but instead refers to a person who contributes to a particular cause. The word *unprofitable* is a Greek word meaning to be *useless* and would refer to someone who does nothing to merit appreciation or reward.

In Revelation 7, after John observed the 144,000 men sealed, he then saw the throne room in heaven and a multitude in white robes who had "come out of great tribulation" and "washed their robes and made them white in the blood of the Lamb" (Rev. 7:14). The idea of washing one's garment implies there were stains on their garment of righteousness. In a parable of the king's son's wedding, a man entered the wedding without a proper garment. The fellow was exposed and forcibly removed from the wedding (Matt. 22:10-13).

In the tribulation, multitudes who were not part of the over-coming remnant of believers will be permitted in the kingdom by death through refusing the mark and the worship of the beast. Thus many shall willingly die for Christ and later be raised to rule with Him. These will serve Christ on earth in different forms of ministry or administrative positions, as they reign with Christ (Rev. 20:4). The Greek word *reign* refers to ruling as a king reigns. Christ will be "King of kings" on earth for 10 centuries, or a thousand years!

The third group in the kingdom will be both the pre-flood genera-tions from Adam to Noah and the post-flood generations, from Noah until the climax of the Law and the prophets, which peaked at the time of the Crucifixion when the new redemptive covenant of Christ was introduced. Christ alluded to the three first patriarchs when he said:

> "And I say to you that many will come from the east and west, and sit down with Abraham, Isaac and Jacob in the kingdom of heaven."
>
> – MATTHEW 8:11 (NKJV)

The prophet Daniel lived in what theologians refer to as the time of the "first Covenant," which was the time of the Law of Moses. About

2,600 years before the crucifixion of Christ, Daniel saw into the heavenly temple and described those surrounding the throne in worship:

> "I beheld, and the same horn (the Antichrist) made war with the saints, and prevailed against them; until the Ancient of days came, and judgment was given to the saints of the most High; and time came that the saints possessed the kingdom."
>
> – DANIEL 7:21-22

> "I beheld till the thrones were cast down, and the Ancient of days did sit, whose garment was white as snow, and the hair of his head like the pure wool: his throne was like the fiery flame, and his wheels as burning fire. A fiery stream issued and came forth from before him: thousand thousands ministered unto him, and ten thousand times ten thousand stood before him: the judgment was set, and the books were opened."
>
> – DANIEL 7:9-10

These "ten thousands," mentioned in Daniel are also alluded to by John as "ten thousand times ten thousand and thousands of thousands" (Rev. 5:11). Both Daniel and John observed the same heavenly scene, with people from the Old Testament (Daniel's day) and the New Testament (John's day) united around the throne. Jude also saw this multitude when he wrote that, "The Lord is coming with ten thousands of his saints to execute judgment on the earth..." (Jude 14). Jude and Daniel used the words "saints," which refers to the holy ones who are consecrated to God. Today we would call these "righteous ones," or "believers and followers of the Messiah." Some of these saints are the descendants of Abraham from the Old Testament.

The fourth group under divine assignment are born again believers who followed Christ, from the initiation of His ministry up to the very minute when He returns to snatch the living and the dead saints, and present them to His Father in the heavenly Temple, where they will worship, be judged at the judgment seat of Christ, and attend the marriage supper of the Lamb (Rev. 11:18; 19:7-9). Those who are part of the *first resurrection* shall serve as priests unto God. There is a heavenly priesthood of which Christ is presently the High Priest, and there will be an earthly priesthood where Christ serves as Priest and

King in a massive temple to be constructed at the beginning of His rule on earth.

Each of the four different groups is part of the "Kingdom of God and the kingdom of heaven." The heavenly kingdom includes the heavenly Temple, Paradise, the New Jerusalem, and the martyrs' paradise; whereas the Kingdom of God is the earthly aspect of Christ's rule, presently through His church during the dispensation of God's grace and later in the millennial reign.

In the Scriptures there are two sacred temples: one is in heaven where God has positioned His throne. The second is on earth in Jerusalem, and will be built under Christ's supervision in the millennial reign. The detailed dimensions of the earthly temple are recorded in Ezekiel chapters 44 through 48. John explained that the 144,000 Jewish men will serve God "in His temple," and the one who "sits upon the throne will dwell among them" (Rev. 7:15). The throne of *Christ* will be on earth for one thousand years, but the throne of *God* will remain in heaven during this time. John said, "These men are before the throne...day and night..." (Rev. 7:15). Christ will also care for them, wiping tears from their eyes, which is a promise to all believers, once the heavenly city New Jerusalem comes down to earth (Rev. 21:4).

All those who willing died during the tribulation will be resurrected from the dead at the conclusion of the tribulation (perhaps near the time of the Marriage Supper) and will rule on earth with Christ for one thousand years (see Rev. 20:4). Their resurrection seems to be alluded to in Daniel 12:2—a resurrection which occurs at the conclusion of the tribulation. Daniel explained:

> "And many of those who sleep in the dust of the earth shall awake, some to everlasting life, some to shame and everlasting contempt."
>
> – Daniel 12:2 (NKJV)

Based on the chronology of Gabriel's explanation given to Daniel, and the fact that this resurrection will occur at the conclusion of Israel's day of trouble, those at this particular resurrection will be raised to life or raised to eternal condemnation (meaning sent into hell). Since one of the resurrected groups is those beheaded who are raised to rule with Christ, the others who are resurrected to "shame and contempt" will be those who accepted the mark of the beast or worshipped the beast and are condemned to hell, along with the beast and false prophet. These martyrs are part of the kingdom of Christ, and will rule with Christ from Jerusalem.

Believers who were found faithful at Christ's coming are blessed to be part of the "first resurrection" (Rev. 20:6). When we return to earth to rule with Christ, we are given specific assignments and positions in the kingdom that will be rewarded by Christ himself, based upon our works during our lifetime. At the Bema, called the *judgment seat of Christ* (Rom. 14:10; 2 Cor. 5:10), we will be judged for our works and words, which will provide Christ our judge the needed information to either reward us or not. For some at this judgment, their foundation of works will come forth as gold, silver and precious stones; for others, their works will be consumed like wood, hay or stubble (1 Cor. 3:12-14). We will be rewarded for our good deeds on earth, only if those deeds can endure the fire of God's judgment.

Rewards that were originally prepared for one person can actually be lost and given to another. Christ warned believers in Revelation not to let any man "take your crown" (Rev. 3:11). This warning was given to a faithful congregation called the Church of Philadelphia. According to John, this church was given an "open door" and Christ wanted them to go through this ministry opportunity door. In this church the strength of some was waning, as some were not moving towards their opportunity due to fear. Christ warned that if they not go through this door of ministry, they could lose their crown (reward).

When we are given an earthly assignment for missions, ministry, preaching the gospel, or caring for others and refuse to move through the doors of opportunity, someone else will be raised up to replace us and, at the Judgement Seat of Christ, that person will receive the reward that would have been ours.

ASSIGNMENTS IN HEAVEN

Angels have been activated in heaven from the beginning of time for numerous purposes. The Scripture indicates that specific angels were created to continually worship God. These angels are stationed in the heavenly throne room and were observed by Isaiah (6:1-3) and John (Rev. 4:6-9). They repeat the same words, echoing back and forth, "Holy, holy, holy, is the Lord God Almighty..." Other angels form heavenly armies that are commissioned to report activities from earth back to heaven (Gen. 18:17-21). One angelic category is identified as ministering spirits (Heb. 1:14), whose responsibilities can include bringing messages from God to His followers (Luke 1:19, 26); assisting in battling demon spirits (Dan. 10:1-13); bringing healing (John 5:1-4); and transporting believers' spirits from earth to heaven at death (Luke 16:22). Never does a moment pass when multitudes of angels are not ministering both in the heavenly and earthly realms.

When believers pass from this life and enter the dimension of heaven, they are escorted into a garden called paradise (a heavenly Garden of Eden). There is not a lot of biblical information to describe what activities these human spirits are engaged in. Paul wrote that he heard things while in paradise that were not lawful to speak of (2 Cor. 12:1-4). While Scripture does not elaborate much on paradise, I am certain there are gardens of flowers, trees, buildings, and a countless multitude of people to meet. However, when we pass from earth to heaven, we are told we to enter into our rest, meaning that we cease from our mental and spiritual laboring (Heb. 4:3-10).

There have been godly individuals who died in an accident, or on the operating table, or otherwise faced a near death experience. Some testify to traveling in their spirit to heaven and seeing the heavenly realities that are yet to be seen and enjoyed. Years ago, my dear friend Pastor Tommy Bates had a marvelous experience in which he was walking through a region of the heavenly paradise, whose geography looked identical to the beautiful hills of his home state of Kentucky. There he met a man who was hand-carving a piece of furniture— one of the most beautiful pieces he had ever seen. After admiring his work, the man told Tommy that he could have it. Tommy replied that he couldn't take it and commented on the time it must have taken to work on this piece. The man let Tommy know that he could make another one, as there were no time limitations in heaven!

When we say that a person desires to "rest," the word brings different images to different people. For some, resting means to lie down and take a quick nap. For others it is connected with a week-end when they are not working. For some, resting is relaxation through outdoor adventures such as fishing or sports, or working on a creative hobby. Activities in heaven do not include reclining on clouds, popping grapes in your mouth for a snack, and listening to a concert by cherubs playing golden harps. This is the image reflected from someone's imagination. There will be things to do when a person passes from this life and rests in the heavenly paradise. I believe you will not only be able to enjoy certain activities you enjoyed on earth, but if there is a gift you desired, such as the ability to sing and keep harmony, it will be imparted to you in heaven. I enjoyed art, drawing, and painting when I was in school, and I made straight A's in class. However, I could not paint a portrait that could satisfy me. I did paint one of George Washington and made an A, but it looked to me more like George *the cartoon* Washington. Should I pass away and not be alive at the coming of the Lord, I hope there are classes for artists, and perhaps I can take the class and paint a beautiful portrait of Christ.

My wife Pam is the most gifted cook that I know. In our conferences, hundreds of people will stand in line to order one of her homemade chicken pot pies, or her homemade vegetable soup, and she could win a blue ribbon with her chicken and dumplings. There are about three desires on her bucket list, and one of those is to take a class from a professional chef. None of us who know her well believe she needs any cooking lessons. However, if she passes before Christ's return and there is a chef's section in paradise, I'm sure when she arrives, she will be found there often. Pam also enjoys growing flowers in the back yard, so she will enjoy the many colorful gardens in paradise.

Some who have experienced visions of paradise have commented that they saw the souls of the righteous gathered together playing instruments. Children were playing with other children. The land was similar to earth, except that the mountains, trees, flowers and grass seem to have energy of their own and burst with more color combinations than on earth. Some say that even the trees emit a sound of praise. Just as the Garden of Eden contained one river that divided into four different rivers, heaven has a river of sparkling crystal water that flows from God. In the New Jerusalem, we find a river of water of life, as well as the tree of life that bears twelve different types of fruit each month (Rev. 22:1-2).

Scripture indicates that the departed righteous souls who now await the resurrection in the heavenly paradise will be the first ones to know the very moment that Christ is returning to earth to transform believers who are alive and catch them up for the gathering together. Paul revealed that the dead in Christ will rise first (1 Thess. 4:16). He revealed an important fact when he said, "For we believe that Jesus died and rose again, even so them which sleep in Jesus will God bring with him," and "We who are alive and remain will not precede those who are asleep" (or who have died – 1 Thess. 4:14-15). The eternal souls of the righteous presently rest in paradise, in the third heaven.

Christ is presently seated at the right hand of God in heaven, and only the heavenly Father knows the exact day and hour when Christ will return (Matt. 25:13). When the fullness of time arrives (Eph. 1:9-10), Christ will gather all of the righteous souls from the heavenly paradise and instantly transport them to earth, where they will be miraculously clothed in a new resurrected body. They will then be gathered in the air, and we will be changed from a mortal body of flesh to an immortal, eternal being and will meet them in the air. From that moment, "So shall we ever be with the Lord" (1 Thess. 4:17). Being with the Lord refers to being with Christ in heaven for a season, and afterward returning to earth with Him to rule.

The resurrection at Christ's return is designated for the "dead in Christ" (1 Thess. 4:17), meaning those who have died in Christ from the moment after His resurrection to the moment He returns to raise the dead. I do not believe this includes any of the Old Testament believers, as this multitude was led by Christ out of the underworld of hades at His resurrection. Some of these saints were seen by many when they walked the streets the same day Christ was raised. We read:

> "And graves were opened; and many bodies of the saints which slept arose, and came out of their graves after His resurrection and went into the holy city and were seen of many."
>
> – MATT. 27:52-53

These raised saints are from the Old Covenant and are presently in heaven, awaiting *not a resurrection*, but the earthly kingdom of the Messiah, which will emerge when Christ returns to rule on earth for a thousand years. This is when Abraham, Isaac, and Jacob will sit down in the kingdom and David will rule Jerusalem from a throne in the Holy City, which at that time will be the spiritual and political capital of the world (Matt. 8:11; Ezek. 34:23-24; Ezek. 37:24-25).

SAINTS RULING ON EARTH

As stated previously, the New Covenant believers will not spend eternity in heaven. We will be presented rewards if we were faithful in our earthly duties and calling, and we will be seated at the marriage supper in heaven while the great tribulation is transpiring on earth (Rev. 11:18; 19:7-9). At the conclusion of the great tribulation, also known as the "day of the Lord" (1 Thess. 5:2; 2 Pet. 3:10), Christ will return, expel Satan and his demonic influence, and set up His earthly kingdom for a thousand years. The global destruction caused by the tribulation, wars, and plagues will then conclude, as the new kingdom of Christ initiates a rebuilding program with Jerusalem as the global headquarters.

During the ten centuries when Christ rules, nations will be reestablished, as resurrected believers from all ages of history will be assigned over the cities, towns and large communities, positioned as mayors, governors, spiritual and political leaders, and directing toward righteousness the tribulation survivors and future generations who repopulate the earth. This will be one of the numerous assignments of Christ's followers when they return from heaven to earth.

In Christ's parable of the nobleman, he delivered his estate to his servants to both oversee and expand while he traveled on a long journey. In this parable the servants were given different amounts of money to invest. Those who invested successfully and multiplied their master's income were rewarded by ruling over multiple cities. However, one of the nobleman's servants "hid his Lord's money," and refused to invest it. He was not only rebuked by the nobleman, but the amount he was entrusted with was taken from him and given to another servant who had been successful in multiplying his Lord's finances (see Luke 19:12-26). The manner in which you fulfill God's will for your life, the number of people you lead to Christ, and your investment in time and finances for the work of God can help determine your level of reward and your new assignment during the millennial reign.

The prophets spoke of this glorious time of the Messiah's rule, and also named different nations in existence at that time. Isaiah described a major highway that will begin in Egypt and extend through Israel all the way into Assyria—which is modern Syria. Both of these nations will join as one with Israel, as Israel's promised borders extend from the River of Egypt to the Euphrates (Gen. 15:18). Zechariah indicated that *all nations* will participate in the yearly Festival of Tabernacles, under the warning of divine retribution if they refuse to attend this festival (Zech. 14:16-19).

Throughout the earth today, billions of people have jobs—ranging from leadership positions, agriculture, building construction, management and so forth. During the thousand year reign, the leadership and ruling positions are rewarded to the faithful saints who will help oversee the global Messianic kingdom. As stated, Jerusalem will be the capital, and the government will be a monarchy, under the kingship of Christ, who will be the "King of kings" (Rev. 17:14; 19:16). All nations must obey the instruction emerging from Jerusalem or they will be punished. A yearly festival, the Feast of Tabernacles, will bring the nations to Jerusalem to celebrate the Messianic kingdom. Any nation refusing to participate will not receive rain on their crops the following year (see Zechariah 14:16-19).

In a resurrected body, there will be no travel restrictions or limitations. Just as angels can maneuver from the third heaven to earth and back without long time restraints, believers in their new bodies can access the heavenly and earthly regions through the power of their will and thought.

However, if we think that we will "live forever in heaven with Christ," we are basing this on man's tradition and often on the songs we heard sung growing up. In reality, heaven will come down to a new earth at the conclusion of the millennial reign and great white throne judgment. All righteous souls will dwell in this Holy City for eternity, which is time without end, as the city will come down from God out of heaven and sit on the new earth (see Rev. 21 and 22).

As I child I assumed I would be bored living in an eternal state. I have long since changed my mind. There will be nothing boring about the future of a believer in covenant with Christ!

When we journey back to ages past, it is startling to see how the fall of one anointed cherub and a third of the angels affected God's creation. However, God already created a redemptive strategy. He already initiated a plan for our permanent return to the original paradise that Adam lost. If you are in covenant with Christ, there are exciting times and a wonderful life ahead—in the world to come.

CHAPTER 17

Access to the Kingdom of Heaven

THERE IS A book in heaven, the city registry in which your name must appear in order to gain permanent access to heaven and reside in the New Jerusalem. When Christ's disciples were casting spirits from those possessed, these newly assigned exorcists were impressed with their authority to command demons out of a human body.

Christ immediately recalled in ages past the moment Satan was cast from heaven, when He told His disciples, "I beheld Satan as lightning fall from heaven" (Luke 10:18). Christ was remembering the original expulsion of evil from the abode of righteousness, the heavenly temple. He then revealed that the secret of defeating these spirits was the authority He had imparted to them (Luke 10:19). Christ said not to rejoice because demons were subject unto them, but rejoice because their names were written in heaven (Luke 10:20).

Exorcism of demons from humans was a continual reminder of the original casting out of Satan and his angels from God's celestial realm. The disciples' source of authority over demons was based upon their spiritual position in heaven, as they were known at the throne and their names were inscribed in the kingdom's registry.

Hebrews 12:23 (KJV) reads:

"To the general assembly and the church of the first born who are written in heaven, to God the judge of all and the spirits of just men made perfect."

In the New Testament, the word *written* is used 132 times in the 1611 King James; however, three different Greek words for written are translated with slightly different meanings. Here the word *written* is *apagrofo*, meaning *to write, to enroll, and to enter into records*. The word refers to recording names, property, income, or information in a legal deed. In the Hebrews reference, it refers to names in a registry that identifies legal citizens.

The New Testament calls this registry the "Lamb's book of life," which inscribes the names of all individuals in covenant with Jesus Christ. This heavenly registry was known as far back as the time of Moses, when he told God that if He did not forgive Israel, then God could blot his name out of His book (Exod. 32:32).

David spoke of a heavenly book that tells the number of tears he cried and how all of his bodily parts were known and penned in a heavenly book before he was ever born (Psa. 56:8; 139:16).

ANCIENT REGISTRIES

One of the oldest registries of early civilizations was found in Mesopotamia, in the area where Abraham's family originated, Ur of Chaldea. Years ago tablets were discovered—a religious record called the "tablets of transgression," and the "tablets of destiny." If a citizen's name appeared in the tablets of transgression, it would be blotted out of the tablets of destiny. According to the belief that filtered among those living in that region, each year the gods gathered in a heavenly fate room where each man's deeds and actions were recorded. It must be remembered that, in those early days before and after Noah's flood, all men spoke one language, and thus beliefs and information were easily passed down from generation to generation.

Interestingly, in the Law of Moses during the yearly Day of Atonement (Yom Kippur), the fate of Israel was determined by God. This idea of God watching the actions of people and determining a positive or negative outcome is also seen when the angelic watchers (guardian angels) made a decree against King Nebuchadnezzar of Babylon. He was warned in a dream, and twelve months later his fate was sealed when he was overcome with a complete emotional and physical breakdown, leading him to live seven years in a forest, like a wild animal (Dan. 4).

During the Neo-Assyrian period (745-612 BC), books were kept that recorded the names of the good and bad people within the city. If a person committed a crime, their name would be blotted out of this book and they would lose their citizenship. The names of good people remained.

In ancient Judea, both before Christ and during the Roman period, the most religious Jews lived in that part of Israel. This was the land grant of the tribe of Judah, with the most noted city being Bethlehem, the city of David. This tribe recorded the names of fully qualified citizens in their registry. The Temple in Jerusalem was located on the border of the tribal land grants of Judah and Benjamin. Temple priests also maintained a specific and precise log of records with the names of all priests and their family genealogies. When a young, thirty-year-old Levite passed the test for the priesthood, he was given a white robe and his name was inscribed in the Temple's priestly registry.

From the time of Moses, the Jews held the concept of the Book of Life. The Jewish Mishna reads:

> "Know what is above thee—a seeing eye, a hearing ear, and thy deeds written in a book" (Avot 2:1).

Among the Jewish prayers prayed daily from the Feast of Trumpets to the Day of Atonement is:

> "Remember us unto life, O king who delights in life, and inscribe us in the Book of Life, for thine own sake, O God of life."

The concept of a city registry containing names of good and bad people, with the bad being expunged from the city directory, is both an ancient and Biblical belief.

REMOVED FROM THE HEAVENLY REGISTRY

Among Christians, there has been intense debate about the spiritual condition of a person who has walked in covenant with Christ, but later willfully turned from the faith. This turning from truth has happened among some, from the time of the early church to this present age, and theologians have split opinions about the spiritual state of the backslider. Some suggest that, if the person returns to their former sin life, they were never really saved. Others believe the person remains in covenant from God's perspective, and are simply out of "fellowship" with God, but cannot ever be lost once they have initially repented. Others believe the backslider forfeits their covenant with God, as all Biblical covenants are based upon two individuals—God and the covenant recipient—and there are blessings for obedience to the covenant and punishments for breaking the covenant.

One of the important verses concerning the relationship of a person who has turned from God, the Word, and from the faith are those concerning names inscribed in the Book of Life. All would agree that your name must be inscribed in the book to enter the heavenly city. We read:

> "But there shall by no means enter it anything that defiles, or causes an abomination or a lie, but only those who are written in the Lamb's Book of Life."
>
> – REVELATION 21:27 (NKJV)

However, can your name be blotted out once it has been inscribed? The answer is yes:

> "And if anyone takes away from the words of the book of this prophecy, God shall take away his part from the Book of Life, from the holy city, and from the things which are written in this book."
>
> – REVELATION 22:19 (NKJV)

> "He who overcomes shall be clothed in white garments, and I will not blot out his name from the Book of Life; but I will confess his name before My Father and before His angels."
>
> – REVELATION 3:5 (NKJV)

> "And anyone not found written in the Book of Life was cast into the lake of fire."
>
> – REVELATION 20:15 (NKJV)

This book has existed from the foundation of the world, or from the beginning of creation (Rev. 17:8). Some who believe in predestination, point out that names were written in the book of life from the "foundation of the world" (Rev. 17:8; 13:8), and thus your name is either in the book and you are predestined for heaven, or not in the book and you are predestined for hell. This erroneous teaching completely does away with man's free will to choose and with God's purpose that all men come to know Christ through repentance.

Since God told Jeremiah that he knew him before he was formed in his mother's belly (Jer. 1:5), and David stated that God knew all the members of his body before they were formed (Psa. 137), this implies that either the human spirit of every living being was originally with God before being placed into the womb at conception, or the book from the foundation of the world has every living human's name in the book. If you choose Christ, your name will remain; or if you reject Christ and His covenant, your name is blotted out.

When growing up in a Full Gospel church, we were taught that a person could backslide and eventually die without Christ. I remember having a fear that if I did one thing wrong, an angel with a giant eraser would erase my name, but by repenting, my name would be restored.

If a person's name is in the book, and they sin, when is their name blotted out? The answer may be found in the warning Christ gave the church at Thyatira. A female was teaching and yet committing fornication with men in the congregation. We read, *"And I gave her space to repent of her fornication; and she repented not"* (Rev. 2:21). The word *space* in Greek is *chronos,* referring to a specific extension of time, not a *set time* but a *period of time.* This space of time is what I call the "grace period," in which a person is given an extended season of mercy to seek God and turn from any disobedience.

This verse indicates that God does not immediately blot out anyone's name if they begin to walk in disobedience. But if they persist in unrepentant sin or iniquity, without seeking God for help, their season of grace will conclude and God can blot their name from the heavenly registry. What is the trigger or the moment of one's name being blotted out?

Two major processes are necessary to enter the covenant of redemption. We are told, "With the heart man believeth unto righteousness and with the mouth confession is made unto salvation" (Rom. 10:10). Two actions are involved with conversion: one is internal and one is external. Faith is internal, being of the heart and mind, while confession is an external expresses of internal beliefs. We overcome Satan by the blood of the Lamb and the word of our testimony (Rev. 12:11). Again, one is an internal application—the blood of the Lamb—and the other is an external expression of the internal work. In both instances, the words (confession and word of our testimony) are significant when we give public witness to our faith and God's changing power.

Sin begins in the heart, and out of the heart proceeds the issues of life (Matt. 15:19). If a believer continues in unrepentant sin, then eventually his confession will change. Instead of saying, "I believe what God said," he will confess, "I don't believe all of that." The combination of actions and words contrary to the obedience of God and His Word are indicators of a person looking back, or backsliding. The backslidden condition eventually separates a person from fellowship and relationship. Unless the backslider returns to God, the person's eternal destiny can be in danger.

CONFESSING BEFORE THE ANGELS

At the judgment, if we have a covenant with Christ, He will confess us before the angels in heaven:

> "Also I say to you, whoever confesses Me before men, him the Son of Man also will confess before the angels of God. But he who denies Me before men will be denied before the angels of God."
>
> – LUKE 12:8-9 (NKJV)

Why are angels involved at *our judgment*? Angels are assigned guardianship and authority to minister to, protect, and give warning to believers. Throughout the Bible, angels served God as messengers to bring heavenly revelation into the earthly realm. Christ did not say the angels would give a report on whether you are a believer or an unbeliever, but that He will confess you before them, if you are a believer.

These angels present at the future judgment are the same who remained loyal to God in the beginning, when all things were being created. All angelic beings were created at or near the same time, and all were created before Adam and Eve. These faithful angels can be identified as "the elect angels" (1 Tim 5:21), meaning *favorite or chosen* angels. All witnessed the ultimate rebellion against God that led to the fall of Satan and the morning stars, yet these two-thirds (Rev. 12:4) remained faithful and loyal to the Creator.

The Book of Life has existed in heaven from the foundation of the world. It is uncertain if the names of the angels were once placed in this book; and if so, when the rebellion occurred, if Satan and the angels that followed him were removed or blotted out from some heavenly registry. If this is possible, it may explain the importance of Christ confessing in front of the holy angels those who never denied Him. This confession is public testimony that the person's name is in the Book of Life.

Remember, the self-appointed assignment Satan pursues is to accuse the saints before God continually. But any accusation void of evidence is a false charge that cannot stand in the heavenly court.

Who *will not* be allowed access to the Holy City, the New Jerusalem? Revelation 21:8 (NKJV) tells us:

> "But the cowardly, unbelieving, abominable, murderers, sexually immoral, sorcerers, idolaters, and all liars shall have their part in the lake which burns with fire and brimstone, which is the second death."

For those who *will be* allowed access to the New Jerusalem, John writes:

> "And God will wipe away every tear from their eyes; there shall be no more death, nor sorrow, nor crying. There shall be no more pain, for the former things have passed away. Then He who sat on the throne said, 'Behold, I make all things new.' And He said to me, 'Write, for these words are true and faithful.' And He said

to me, 'It is done! I am the Alpha and the Omega, the Beginning and the End. I will give of the fountain of the water of life freely to him who thirsts. He who overcomes shall inherit all things, and I will be his God and he shall be My son.' "

– REV. 21:4-7 (NKJV):

"But there shall by no means enter it anything that defiles, or causes an abomination or a lie, but only those who are written in the Lamb's Book of Life."

– REV. 21:27 (NKJV)

Imagine the sorrow of those being cast into the lake of fire, knowing they rejected Christ and wasted their life on earth, and now there is no second chance! The most important decision you will make in this life is to repent of your sins and accept the redemptive work of Christ, and allow Him to transform your life as you continue to walk in His ways.

The sweetest sound we will ever hear is, "Well done, good and faithful servant; enter into your rest." May your name be found written in the Lamb's Book of Life, and may you too walk upon the sacred mountain!

CHAPTER 18

Important Answers to Tough Questions

Question: Can you elaborate more on the link between Satan being cast out of heaven during the construction of the heavenly Jerusalem and why this would cause such hatred for Israel and Jerusalem today?

Answer: For centuries, the Jewish people have been the most persecuted, despised and hated ethnic group on the plant. This hatred is so intense during seasons of persecution, that the root motivation obviously has its source in satanic strategies assigned to destroy Israel and the Jews.

This hatred of the Hebrew race may stem from several spiritual facts. First, it was the Israelite tribal family that was given the first promise, through Abraham, of a nation (Israel) that would be God's chosen nation, birthed by His sovereign plan—a nation in which all the nations of the earth would be blessed (Gen. 12:3; 22:18). Centuries following Abraham, the first written revelation of God's spiritual, moral, social and judicial laws were revealed to Moses, requiring Israel's obedience to maintain their special status. These "rules of heaven," inked in the Torah, would become the foundational guidelines for Israel. Centuries later, they forged the foundational principles in Gentile nations (such as England and America) whose founders read, understood, and practiced the words of the Bible.

The men of Israel alone were given circumcision as the physical mark of the covenant (Gen 17:11). Israel was destined to be the nation from which the Messiah would emerge, as Christ had a Jewish mother whose linage was the tribe of Judah and whose home was Bethlehem, the city of David. Thus the Jewish nation brought forth the Redeemer who would crush the kingdom of Satan.

God revealed the Tabernacle to Moses, patterned after the temple in heaven. Moses and his selected men constructed on earth a structure that existed in heaven, thus bringing a little heaven on earth for God's chosen people. The Tabernacle provided a new opportunity for God to directly commune with His people after the fall of Adam and Eve. God used one mediator called the high priest who, once a year on the Day of Atonement, met with God at the Ark of the Covenant in the Holy of Holies (see Lev. 16). Israel's Tabernacle in the wilderness and later Temple in Jerusalem enabled God to gain personal access to mankind through offerings, ritual sacrifices, and prayers.

Both the Tabernacle and the Temple concealed rituals and offerings that were a type and shadow of man's future redemption. Perhaps this is why Satan desired that the Babylonians destroy Jerusalem and the Temple, and then seventy years later attempt to hinder the reconstruction of the Temple and city by using leaders from Samaria (see Ezra and Nehemiah).

As for Jerusalem, when King David captured the stronghold of Zion, also called Jebus (2 Sam. 5:7; Judg. 19:10), he moved the political headquarters of Israel from Hebron to a new political and spiritual capital named Jerusalem. God said He would place His name on this city and mark it above all the cities on earth (Deut. 12:5, 11, 21). When David's son Solomon built Israel's first Temple, God's presence (the cloud of His glory) manifested among the priests in Jerusalem. God had marked the mountains of Moriah in Jerusalem as the site of the Temple and the future hill where Christ would die (Gen. 22:2; 2 Chron. 3:1). Thus Jerusalem is the city of God, His holy mountain, and the place where Satan met his ultimate defeat when Christ rose from the dead!

When Satan hears the name Jerusalem, perhaps he is reminded of the heavenly city he never completed, his expulsion from the heavenly temple, and the fact that God used the Jews, Israel and Jerusalem to protect and select a righteous seed that gave birth to the Messiah, Jesus Christ, who would destroy Satan's kingdom of darkness. The ability of Jerusalem to still exist despite destructions and countless occupations proves that God exists. The inability of Satan to annihilate the Jews, using two destructions (the Babylonians and Romans), severe persecutions, and the death of six million Jews during the Holocaust also reveals God's favor upon His covenant people. Jerusalem is and will be in the millennium the eternal city.

The continuous existence of the Jews, Israel and Jerusalem is a daily reminder that Satan's doom is sealed and his final season on earth is linked to the city and the people. When prophetic events unfold, Satan knows he "has but a short time" (Rev. 12:12). He will initiate one final attempt during the last half of the tribulation to eradicate the Jews from the earth, but that attempt, like all others, will fail.

The earthly Jerusalem is a sore reminder to Satan of his past. It is also a reminder that his future doom is sealed when Christ returns to Jerusalem (Rev. 20:1-4).

Question: In the divine foreknowledge of God, He knew that Satan would rebel and that Adam would disobey His instructions and be expelled from the garden. To prevent Adam from sinning, why didn't God just destroy Satan after he rebelled, so that Adam and Eve would not have been tempted? Why was the adversary permitted to influence Adam and Eve in the Garden of Eden?

Answer: This question has been asked for centuries. Certainly, God has foreknowledge of all things, including each person's physical birth and planned destiny (Psa. 139:13-16; Jer. 1:5; Gal.1:15). The word *foreknowledge* is mentioned twice in the New Testament, in Acts 2:23 and 1 Pet. 1:2. The Greek word foreknowledge is *prognosis*, from a root word meaning *to know something, such as an outcome, in advance.* God knew the outcome before He created both Lucifer and Adam. Redemption was pre-planned before Adam's creation as indicated by John who wrote that Christ was "the lamb slain from the foundation of the world" (Rev. 13:8). God foreknew Adam's failure and made arrangements in advance for all of mankind's redemption. This redemptive plan is further proven when, immediately after Adam and Eve sinned in the garden, God released the first Messianic prophecy, indicating the seed of the women would bruise the head of the serpent (Gen. 3:15).

As to why God did not immediately *destroy* Satan along with the rebellious angels, the Almighty did prepare a place of eternal confinement called hell for these spirit rebels. Christ stated that hell was prepared for the devil and his angels (Matt. 25:41). Satan is a cherub, an angel God personally created along with all the angelic hosts, including the sinful remnant that turned and became involved in the heavenly uprising. All created angels are spirit beings (Heb. 1:7) with certain features that mark them in specific categories (archangels, seraphim, cherub, living creatures, and so forth).

Satan's self-exaltation led to his expulsion from heaven, long before God formed Adam in Eden. Satan's acts of resistance and disobedience to God introduced something to the future world called free will. Planted in the Garden of Eden were two opposing trees—one that energized and renewed life, and the other that introduced death and separation. One tree was blessed and the other cursed, and God's warning of death by disobedience was known to both Adam and Eve (Gen. 2:17; 3:3). The first couple was given the power to *choose* between good or evil, right or wrong, and life or death, because of free will. Just as some angels chose Satan over God, man also would be given a choice of whom he would serve.

Free will continues to this present age. God's kingdom is a theocracy, not a dictatorship. God does not force people to serve Him, nor does He prevent people from serving Him. However, disobedience has serious consequences. When Adam chose death over life, he cursed humanity, as by "one man sin entered the world and death by sin, so death passed upon all men ..." (Rom. 5:12). Even when a sinner accepts Christ and becomes a believer, they retain their power to make decisions, including the power of choice.

Adam's sin gave Satan and his kingdom legal permission to retain influence over succeeding generations as the tempter (Matt. 4:3) and accuser of the righteous (Rev. 12:10). Any people who hear and refuse the Gospel message of redemption will be confined in the same dark underworld where the fallen angels have been assigned (Matt. 8:12; 22:13). A spirit being cannot be burned to death or destroyed, and at death it is either brought into God's presence or separated from Him at death. Fallen angels are forever separated from God, as will be all sinners who reject the New Covenant of Christ. Good and evil will co-exist on earth as long as Satan and his rebels are free to exercise their authority. After the great white throne judgment, when Satan is cast into an unescapable burning prison, God's plan of perfection for His creation will come full circle and be as it was intended in the beginning.

In summary, God in his foreknowledge knew the failure and rebellion coming in both heaven and on earth; so He planned a divine restoration from the foundation of the world. It will end the way it began: with no pain, no sorrow, no crying, and no death (Rev. 21:4). In the end, God wins!

Question: Some ministers have been teaching that the followers of all world religions will eventually end up in heaven, as each religion is simply a different path to God. Some say that at the great white throne judgment, only Satan, the antichrist, and the false prophet will be cast into the lake of fire, and all other sinners will be forgiven and enter the eternal kingdom. Is there any truth to this?

Answer: The doctrine called Universalism or Universal Restoration is not new. It was promoted by certain heretics in the early church, and rejected by the recognized Bishops and leaders of the church. The Universalist teaches that Christ's redemptive work was for the whole world, which is correct; however, they add their opinion that the whole world is *already saved* but presently they do not know it. This teaching takes certain verses and stretches their meaning beyond the intended interpretation. Their four main points are: repentance is not needed through Christ, as heaven is automatic for all people; man is already saved and heaven bound but does not know it; there is no need to preach or convert from any other religion, as all religions eventually end up in the same heaven; and hell does not exist, thus no one is going there.

To promote universalism, certain "proof texts" are used, such as, "He is the Savior of all men..." (1 Tim. 4:10); "...I will draw all men unto me" (John 12:32); "...in Christ all men are made alive..." (1 Cor. 15:22). The phrase "all men" is interpreted to mean that all men (all sinners and all people of other religions) are, at this moment, being made alive, already saved, and will be drawn to Christ.

However, Christ placed a major condition on anyone who would be saved and that is, "whosoever believeth" (John 3:16). Two verses that dismantle the heresy of Universal Restoration are: "God commands all men to repent" (Acts 17:30), and men are "without Christ, being aliens from the commonwealth of Israel, and strangers of the covenant of promise, having no hope, and without God in the world" (Eph. 2:12). Heaven is guaranteed only to those who repent, believe and confess Christ, as Paul instructed that we must "confess with our mouth and believe with our heart" to be saved (Rom. 10:9).

If all people from all religions are already saved and will enter heaven, then why was it necessary for Christ to die on the cross and resurrect? Was it just to form another religion? If salvation is automatic and everybody is already heaven bound, then why were ten disciples willing to die as martyrs for the message of Christ they preached? Why did thousands of early Christians die in ten major persecutions initiated by Roman emperors?

Christ commanded His followers to go into all the world, preaching, baptizing, making disciples, and warning that those who do not believe will be condemned (Mark 16:15-16). There would be no need for any of that if all mankind will end up in heaven despite their sins, idolatry, and iniquity. One verse plainly states that there will be a separation in eternity between the righteous and the unrighteous. We read in Revelation 22:14-15:

> "Blessed are those who do His commandments that they may
> have the right to the tree of life, and may enter through the gates
> into the city. But outside *are* dogs and sorcerers and sexually

immoral and murderers and idolaters, and whoever loves and practices a lie."

Heaven is for the repentant and the righteous who have been redeemed by the Covenant of Christ.

Question: One teaching within the Body of Christ states that once the great white throne judgment occurs and God casts Satan, his angels, and sinners into the lake of fire, all sinners will experience annihilation and cease to exist. Is this true?

Answer: The great white throne judgment, referred to by John in Revelation 20:11, includes all sinners—from Adam's descendants to all unsaved who died on earth through the final day of the millennial reign of Christ (Rev. 20:4). The souls of all sinners who have died without a redemptive covenant and without repenting of their sins are now confined in a massive underground chamber located deep under the crust of the earth. When this heavenly judgment begins at the end of the one-thousand-year rule of Christ, hell will empty out the hosts of fallen angels (2 Pet. 2:4; Jude 6), along with sinners from all nations throughout world history.

At this judgment, those who have been brought out of hell will know why they did not enter the kingdom, as their deeds were recorded in heavenly books and will be exposed before all in the heavenly court.

When this judgment concludes, death and hell are cast into the lake of fire. As alluded to in this book, death and hell are not just theological terms or metaphors, but are actual spirits active on earth since the fall of Adam. This *duo of destruction* will be thrown into the "lake burning with fire and brimstone" (Rev. 20:15). The underworld of hell does consist of fire; however, the lake of fire is a different place from the hell chamber.

At this judgment, heavenly books detailing the deeds (works) of these individuals are opened and each person will be judged according to the records. Any person whose name is not in the book of life will be confined in the lake of fire. Any sinner originally placed in hell was sentenced to confinement because their name was not written in the book of life.

Notice that both hell and death deliver up the dead. Those who lived and died during the thousand-year reign of Christ must appear at this judgment, including any tribulation survivors who might have received Christ, and those born on earth during the kingdom age of Christ. These people will still be subject to death, as they have an earthy body that must die. These will be raised at the end of the thousand years and stand before God to be judged based on the records of their earthly life. If they served Christ, they will enter the eternal kingdom and live with Him in the New Jerusalem. All others will be condemned and removed from the heavenly throne room and cast into the lake of fire.

The question is, once souls are cast into the lake of fire, will they continually be punished for eternity or will they simply cease to exist? The idea that punishment is only temporary and eventually the soul perishes is often based upon the objection that a just God would never allow a person to be punished eternally. Also, being cast into the lake of fire is called the "second death" (Rev. 20:14). The phrase is interpreted by some to mean that the sinner dies or is annihilated the moment they enter the lake of fire. However, a sinner's *first death* was when a person lived on earth in sin, and "sin brought forth death" (James 1:15). This type of death is not a cessation of the soul, but a separation of the soul from the person's body and a confinement in hell. The *second death* does not refer to the burning of the soul to non-existence. It is a second death in that the soul and spirit are now confined in a different chamber after judgment—not hell, but the lake of fire.

Each human soul and spirit has an eternal component. At physical death, the soul and spirit exit the physical body and join other departed spirits in hell (the unrighteous) or paradise (the righteous). These regions of eternal existence have been the abode of opposing spiritual realms since the death of the first man. For example, Abraham passed away almost 4,000 years ago, being born 1,948 years after Adam's son Seth was born; yet in the future millennium kingdom, men will sit down with Abraham, Isaac and Jacob (Matt. 8:11). Abraham will be in a resurrected body that will never again experience death. Just as with Adam, the human spirit consists of the breath of God that enables us to be a living soul (Gen. 2:7). That which comes from God has an everlasting component, meaning the soul and spirit within each human is eternal and will always exist.

Death, Hell and Satan will be cast into the lake of fire (Rev. 20:10) along with the beast and false prophet (Rev. 19:20). In the statements of Christ, when He spoke of eternal punishment on the disobedient, He used the phrase, "cast into hell fire" and "cast into everlasting fire" (Matt. 18:8-9). When Christ encouraged the righteous, He promised them eternal life and everlasting life (Mk. 10:30; John 3:15-16; 6:47). The phrase *eternal life* is mentioned twenty-six times, and *everlasting life* ten times in the New Testament. Christ spoke of believers who will live forever (John 6:58) and reign forever with Christ (Rev. 22:5).

Forever means forever. Life for a believer is eternal and punishment for a sinner is also eternal. The Greek word used for eternal means perpetual and can allude to the eternal past or the eternal future. God existed in eternity past (or ages past) and will continue to exist in eternity future—a world without end (Eph. 3:21).

Question: Since angels were once perfect yet were able to influence each other to rebel against God, is it possible that once believers enter the New Jerusalem, they too could be tempted to rebel and then the cycle of disobedience would repeat itself?

Answer: The first point is that God did not create Satan as an evil entity, as "God cannot be tempted with evil neither tempts he any man" (James 1:13); neither did He create the seed of wickedness to plant as seed thoughts in angelic rebels. The Bible teaches that Satan, as a created angel, was perfect until iniquity was found in him (Ezek. 28:15). This iniquity began as a seed and grew into an act, just as all sin begins as a seed. The Word says that, "When lust is conceived it brings forth sin...." (James 1:15). There is a moment when the thought becomes a seed and the seed matures to produce negative fruit.

In our present condition we dwell in flesh and blood bodies and live in a carnal world that is influenced by evil men and spirit rebels (Eph. 6:12). All men are subject to like passions (James 5:17) and are capable of being tempted to the point of yielding to sin. Temptation that leads to actions contrary to God's Word is possible as long as we dwell in these houses of clay. In Romans 7, Paul wrote of the clash between a sinful and righteous nature within each person and how this spiritual conflict becomes a struggle in every person. However, Paul wrote of a time when he would be delivered from the body of this death (Rom. 7:24).

The struggle of temptation and sin will cease when the soul and spirit are released from the body. At the coming of Christ and the resurrection of the dead in Christ, each person will transition from a mortal to an immortal body, fitted with the glory of God (1 Cor. 15:50-54). When believers receive their resurrected bodies, Paul said we will be the "spirits of just men made perfect" (Heb. 12:23). This perfection includes freedom from the potential and power of sin. Sin will have no rule or dominion over us.

From a New Testament perspective, once the resurrection of the righteous dead occurs, there is no record of any type of rebellion, resistance or sin problem among the righteous men and women who will have been raised and given a new body. Satan currently influences the weak flesh, as "our spirit is willing but our flesh is weak" (Mark 14:38). Once we enter the heavenly kingdom, rule on earth with Christ, and enter the New Jerusalem for eternity, all forces of Satan, demons, and evil will be forever removed. The influence and power of the tempter to work his wickedness on humanity will cease.